FROM PAIN to PEACE

Help for Parents with Wayward Children

FROM PAIN to PEACE

Help for Parents with Wayward Children

SHARON CLONTS & JANICE CHALKER

BOOKCRAFT
Salt Lake City, Utah

Library of Congress Catalog Card Number: 93-70862
ISBN 0-88494-879-X

First Printing, 1993

Printed in the United States of America

To our mother

Blanche McCue

Contents

Acknowledgments

Several people have contributed support and skills to the development of the manuscript that has now become this book.

We are most grateful to those who have provided their very personal experiences for publication. These stories appear in the book in italic type. Names and sometimes circumstances have been altered to protect privacy, but the integrity of the story has always been preserved.

We express deep appreciation to Mathew Chalker for his constant encouragement and for his many suggestions and improvements. We similarly thank Roy Clonts for his support and generous assistance during the long haul. Likewise we express loving gratitude to our children for their patience and support.

We appreciate the helpful editorial suggestions made by Marjorie Eddy, Joel McCue, and Sharon Elwell.

Our thanks go also to the involved members of Bookcraft's staff, especially to Diane Orton, who first saw the book's potential; to Cory Maxwell for his kind encouragement; and to George Bickerstaff for his skilled and patient editing.

Introduction

A close friend once confided: "I'm so discouraged; I just don't know what to do; my daughter's life has been ruined because of the unrighteous decision she has made in her life." For days after learning of her daughter's problems, my friend was overwhelmed by a flood of emotions. She could hardly think straight. There was no comfort—only heartache, grief, and shame.

In her search for answers she picked up what she hoped would be an inspirational book, one that would comfort her broken heart. There she read a story about a mother who had just lost her child to a terrible disease. Grieving beyond relief, she found her comfort when the child appeared to her in spirit form to let her know he was happy and peaceful.

That sweet, inspirational story had just the opposite effect on my friend. She knelt down immediately and sent up a bitter prayer to her Heavenly Father: "There is comfort for this mother, but where is the comfort for mothers like me?"

Concerned loved ones find it difficult to say the right words to a parent who has lost a child through death. What can be done to relieve the pain of a grieving parent who has seemingly lost a child to *spiritual* death?

There is nothing novel about dealing with prodigals; it has

been a shared adversity of parents since Adam and Eve. Today as moral pollution intensifies above the high water marks of corruption and decadence, more and more spiritual casualties occur. Still, knowing that the grief of parents is similar regardless of the time period in which their child wandered, we can look to prophets of all ages for wisdom. It may seem harder today to endure a child's waywardness when we remember what is and has been expected of our generation, as President Ezra Taft Benson has expressed it:

> All through the ages the prophets have looked down through the corridors of time to our day. Billions of the deceased and those yet to be born have their eyes on us. Make no mistake about it—you are a marked generation. There has never been more expected of the faithful in such a short period of time. . . . Never before on the face of this earth have the forces of evil and the forces of good been as well organized. (Ezra Taft Benson, *Speeches of the Year*, 1979, p. 59.)

We need to remember that many of those who stray from the truth may well have been valiant spirits in the premortal life where for a lengthy existence they were used to making correct choices. We should not assume that ten to twenty years of incorrect choices during this probationary state can extinguish that light. We must have hope.

While in many ways the Lord is pouring out his Spirit to individuals as the Church grows, in general the Spirit of the Lord is being withdrawn from the earth as evil and wickedness abound (see D&C 63:32). Values, attitudes, morals, and general conditions of the world are degenerating at an ever-quickening pace. As prophesied, the whole earth is in commotion (see D&C 45:26). The intensity and accelerated pace of this wickedness was dramatically depicted in an Ann Landers column.

> Dear Ann: In the 1940s the major problems that teachers had to deal with were as follows:

—Not getting homework on time.
—Talking during class.
—Making noise.
—Running in the hallways.
—Getting out of place in line.
—Wearing improper clothing.
In the '80s the teachers must contend with:
—Students who are strung out on alcohol and drugs.
—Pregnant girls.
—Suicidal students.
—Threats of rape and murder.
—Stealing.
—Assault.
—Guns and knives in the classroom.
—Arson and bombing.
Scary, isn't it.
(*Los Angeles Times*, August 18, 1988.)

We all tell our own horror stories about how bad things really are in the world. This is the environment in which our youth spend much of their time. Not surprisingly, many Latter-day Saint youth are being drawn into the whirlpool of evil, causing their parents to be loaded down with frustration, anguish, and grief. Many parents have been so badly hurt by turbulence in their homes that their lives are changed for the worse. They are left with scars that are difficult to heal. Often these experiences lead to blame and guilt that destroy the very foundation of the family. Some have become so dysfunctional that they are unable to perform their duties in the home, at work, or at church.

"There's such an overwhelming feeling of failure," says a sister who reflects on her family's experiences with a wayward child. "I review every day from the time he was born and ask myself what happened. What did we do wrong? . . . I have felt a sense of failure to the Church family, too, not just to my own. At first I felt unworthy to serve in my Church calling and I asked to be released." (Sue Bergin, *Ensign*, March 1988, p. 15.)

Today's parents are contending with conditions and problems that used to be unthinkable. It is no wonder some are weary and numb. Our modern prophets have emphasized the challenges of raising a family in today's world. "I recognize," said Elder Gordon B. Hinckley, "that there are parents who, notwithstanding an outpouring of love and a diligent and faithful effort to teach them, see their children grow in a contrary manner and weep while their wayward sons and daughters willfully pursue courses of tragic consequence" (*Ensign*, November 1978, p. 19).

Elder Boyd K. Packer also has addressed this issue:

> It is a great challenge to raise a family in the darkening mists of our moral environment.
>
> We emphasize that the greatest work you will do will be within the walls of your home (see Harold B. Lee, *Ensign*, July 1973, p. 98), and that "no other success can compensate for failure in the home" (David O. McKay, *Improvement Era*, June 1964, p. 445).
>
> The measure of our success as parents, however, will not rest solely on how our children turn out. That judgment would be just only if we could raise our families in a perfectly moral environment, and that now is not possible.
>
> It is not uncommon for responsible parents to lose one of their children, for a time, to influences over which they have no control. They agonize over rebellious sons or daughters. They are puzzled over why they are so helpless when they have tried so hard to do what they should.
>
> It is my conviction that those wicked influences one day will be overruled. (*Ensign*, May 1992, p. 68.)

This book has been fashioned expressly for parents, relatives, friends, and loved ones who are living in the wake of a defiant prodigal. It aspires to kindle hope where there is despair; to revive esteem where there is a sense of shame; to comfort where there is pain; and to share insight, perspective, and understanding.

1

Stop Beating Yourself

We mortals tend to exhibit a destructive way of handling the situation when our ambitions, goals, plans, hopes, or dreams don't unfold according to our expectations, particularly when they involve our children. We tend to become emotionally entangled in the ordeal to the point that our disappointments become personal failures. Because so much can and does go wrong in the execution of our parenting project, almost any failure has the potential to become something to beat ourselves with. As Barbara Smith put it, "Ideals are stars to steer by; they are not a stick to beat ourselves with" (*Ensign*, March 1976, p. 8). A puny stick intensifies into a club when amplified by our knowledge of the eternal significance of our parental stewardship. Unfortunately, if this scenario uncoils, we become, after the prodigal, a second victim in Satan's malignant scheme. When a youngster gets sucked into the horrible abyss of sin, we must not allow ourselves to become drawn into the same void as a victim of despair, grief, shame, or guilt.

Jane attended Brigham Young University, married a returned missionary, raised a large, handsome family, and taught Relief Society while her husband served in the bishopric. She and her husband saw to it that their family attended all their church meetings, held family home

evening every Monday night, and listened to their children; they read
to them at night, gave them chores around the house, and so forth. In
other words, they did all that they could to raise moral, caring, respon-
sible children.

Nevertheless, this same woman watched in horror and despair as
one after another of her children turned away from their teachings to
drugs, immorality, cult religions, and drop-out living. In the end, she
was hardly spared even one child. The pain and hopelessness became
so great that she could not even bring herself to care for her family. In
her mind, she was a total failure. She finally fell into such a state of
deep depression that she withdrew completely into a world of her own
where no one could reach her.

"There is no pain so piercing as that caused by the loss of a
child," said Elder Boyd K. Packer (*Improvement Era*, December
1970, p. 109). A major part of the cutting pain inflicted upon
sorrowing parents when their child becomes wayward is shame
and guilt. For such parents the load is doubled as they deal not
only with their ungovernable child but also with the anguish
that comes from the blame they heap upon themselves: Where
did I go wrong? Was I too hard or too easy? Did I do too much
or too little? Did I lecture instead of listen? What do I do now?
Such parents need to heed the words of Lowell S. Bennion:
"Why be defeated twice, once by our mistakes and again by our
attitude toward them?" (*Improvement Era*, October 1967, p. 12.)

At times, it's hard to determine whether the suffering stems
from the loss of the child or the equally real loss of self-esteem.
Elder Howard W. Hunter remarked:

There are many in the Church and in the world who are living
with feelings of guilt and unworthiness because some of their
sons and daughters have wandered or strayed from the fold. . . .
At the outset we understand that conscientious parents try their
best, yet nearly all have made mistakes. One does not launch
into such a project as parenthood without soon realizing that
there will be many errors along the way. Surely our Heavenly Father knows, when he entrusts his spirit children into the care of

young and inexperienced parents, that there will be mistakes and errors in judgment. (*Ensign*, November 1983, p. 63.)

There are circumstances in which parents have indeed made serious mistakes, particularly parents who have been emotionally or physically abusive to a child. Additionally there are those who through indifference or neglect failed to teach their children to walk "in light and truth" (see D&C 93:39–48). For these parents, repentance and restitution are needed. For most parents, however, dwelling on the past (beyond self-examination) is futile. As Elder Howard W. Hunter suggested: "We should never let Satan fool us into thinking that all is lost. Let us take pride in the good and right things we have done; reject and cast out of our lives those things that are wrong; look to the Lord for forgiveness, strength, and comfort; and then move onward." (*Ensign*, November 1983, p. 65.)

The fact is that all parents are human and have made mistakes. Each parent who has ever existed could have found a stick to beat himself with. Even the great prophets have made errors along the way. They also had to go through the toil of life: they despaired; they were harrowed down in sorrow; they winced with pain; they pleaded with the Lord; they exercised faith, repented, mastered obedience, accumulated knowledge; and they forgave. Probably the reason why we call them great is that they triumphed over their weaknesses. They came to understand that as long as they put complete trust in God they could endure life's experiences.

The prophets learned to manage the inescapable tension between moral agency and intervention as they trained their children. They understood the great gifts of repentance and forgiveness the Savior offers. Their knowledge and faith gave them power to resist the debilitating stress of Satan's temporary victories over their families. Thus, along with the marvelous doctrinal teachings of the scriptures, those records give selective glimpses into some of the prophets' private family experiences, particularly as they grappled with prodigal children.

Jacob: The Great Patriarch

Jacob was the grandson of Abraham and heir to the blessings of the Abrahamic covenant (see Abraham 2:6–11). Nevertheless, Jacob's family proved to be an interminable source of sorrow during his lifetime. His brother, Esau, resented him; his father-in-law deceived him; his wives were jealous of each other; his son was sexually immoral with his concubine; his daughter was raped; his two sons Levi and Simeon avenged her by massacring the male Hivites; and his son Joseph apparently was killed.

Jacob had four wives, but he favored Rachel and her child Joseph. He "loved Joseph more than all his children." When the other sons saw the favoritism toward Joseph "they hated him." Their hatred drove them to sell their younger brother into slavery and then lie to their father. Jacob was inconsolable, "and thus his father wept for him." (Genesis 37:3–4, 35.)

Even though Jacob showed great favoritism toward Joseph, the sin occurred in the way the brothers exercised their agency in their response to Jacob's partial treatment of Joseph. Elder Bruce R. McConkie commented: "Agency underlies all things— all advancement, all progression, even existence itself. It is based on the presence of opposites between which a choice must be made." (*A New Witness for the Articles of Faith* [Salt Lake City: Deseret Book Co., 1985], p. 90.) Each of Jacob's sons was responsible for his own behavior.

Elder Howard W. Hunter has reminded us: "Each of us is unique. Each child is unique. Just as each of us starts at a different point in the race of life, and just as each of us has different strengths and weaknesses and talents, so each child is blessed with his own special set of characteristics." (*Ensign*, November 1983, pp. 64–65.) It was thus with Jacob's sons. Each reacted in his own unique manner. Reuben, the oldest, tried to save Joseph and, by suggesting that they throw him in a pit, managed to prevent the brothers from murdering him. He planned to later rescue him. Judah, on the other hand, with pragmatic reasoning saw a "profit" in selling his younger brother into slavery. (See Genesis 37:18–30.) This, in part, demonstrates the uniqueness of his character.

The Lord's purposes are never thwarted; Joseph eventually prospered and was set over "all the land of Egypt." A famine "over all the face of the earth" brought his brothers before him. (See Genesis 41:41, 56.) Joseph lovingly tested his brothers by threatening to place Benjamin (Jacob's only other son by Rachel) into slavery. The years must have brought remorse and softening to Judah, because it was Judah who stepped forward and offered himself in place of Benjamin.

Besides their cruel trick on Joseph and, in consequence, on their father, the Bible records other ignoble acts done by at least some of these brothers. In the absence of information on the subject, one would hope that, over time, through the atoning sacrifice of Jesus Christ each of these brothers repented, found forgiveness, worked through his problems, and became a true patriarch to his house. In any event, the Lord worked with their posterity, tutored them, counseled them, sent prophets to them, and established a numerous covenant people.

After all had been explained by Joseph, and the ten older men realized that this great man, second only to Pharaoh in power, was in reality the brother they had sold into slavery, Joseph demonstrated the wonderful uniqueness of his character and the true greatness of his soul. With sweet sensitivity he reached out to them with these comforting words: "And God sent me before you to preserve you a posterity in the earth, and to save your lives by a great deliverance. So now it was not you that sent me hither, but God." (Genesis 45:7–8.)

Any one of the shameful acts perpetrated by his sons could have caused Jacob to ask himself, Where did I go wrong? or How did I fail? Jacob's domestic difficulties help us understand that his life of righteousness was of more concern to the Lord than his mistakes and errors of judgment. His value must have been great in the sight of God, because the Savior had no problem with allying his own sacred name to that of this valiant patriarch by referring to himself as the God of Abraham, Isaac, and Jacob (see Matthew 22:32; 1 Nephi 19:10; D&C 136:21).

We are all children of our Father in Heaven, who is pleased with our strivings for righteous living. "Real joy comes from righteous character, and that is built from a pattern of consistent righteous decisions" (Richard G. Scott, *Ensign*, May 1991, p. 34).

Lehi and Sariah: Goodly Parents

Apparently Lehi and Sariah were not perfect parents, either. Nonetheless, they were not culpable for the rebellion of their sons Laman and Lemuel. The vision of the tree of life as recorded in the eighth chapter of 1 Nephi describes a tree and "the exceedingly great joy" that comes from partaking of its fruit. Lehi recounts that he earnestly beckoned to his wife, Sariah, and two of his sons, Sam and Nephi, to join him at the tree. "And . . . they did come unto me and partake of the fruit also" (1 Nephi 8:16).

Lehi desires his other sons Laman and Lemuel to come and partake; he beckons to them, "but they would not come . . . and partake of the fruit" (1 Nephi 8:18). We may see in this prophetic vision that the Lord compassionately rescued Lehi from any misconception of parental negligence regarding his two wayward sons. The vision clearly shows Lehi that his sons rejected the fruits of the tree of life (or the love of God) of their own free will and choice.

In 2 Nephi, father Lehi, knowing his death is near, tries one last time to reason with his rebellious sons. He pleads with them to come back to the Lord so that they will not be cursed and cut off: "My heart hath been weighed down with sorrow from time to time, for I have feared, lest for the hardness of your hearts the Lord your God should come out in the fulness of his wrath upon you, that ye be cut off and destroyed forever. . . . O my sons, that these things might not come upon you." (2 Nephi 1:17, 19.)

However, his ardent pleading fell on deaf ears. Shortly after their father's death, Laman and Lemuel became angry with Nephi and sought again to take his life.

Even though Lehi's heart had been "weighed down with sorrow" for his sons his comprehension that his own exaltation did not rely on their behavior can be seen in his profound statement: "But behold, the Lord hath redeemed my soul from hell; I have beheld his glory, and I am encircled about eternally in the arms of his love" (2 Nephi 1:15). Lehi understood this eternal truth: our heavenly parent recognizes the love and sacrifice we make as parents. Elder Howard W. Hunter has emphasized this truth by saying: "Know that our Heavenly Father will recognize the love and the sacrifice, the worry and the concern, even though our great effort has been unsuccessful. Parents' hearts are ofttimes broken, yet they must realize that the ultimate responsibility lies with the child after parents have taught correct principles." (*Ensign*, November 1983, p. 64.)

King Mosiah: Heartache Over Sons

Mosiah is well known in the scriptures for two reasons. First, he was a noble and righteous Nephite king. Second, he had four sons who became some of the greatest missionaries of all time. We read in the book of Mosiah about the greatness of this monarch. He inherited the throne from his father, King Benjamin, and every reference to Mosiah and his rule reveals a man who was intent only on serving his people, with no interest in gaining power or glory for himself. In fact, it was Mosiah who proposed the plan for the Nephites to be ruled by judges rather than kings. His attitude toward kingship was the opposite of most kings. In this he truly showed the greatness of his character. Moreover, he did all he could within his stewardship as king to build up and prosper the Church of God: he was a mainstay and support to Alma, the high priest of the Church, and he was a good example to the whole kingdom.

While Mosiah was doing all he could to build up the Church of God his own sons "did go about secretly . . . seeking to destroy the church, and to lead astray the people of the Lord." These four prodigal sons probably constituted all of his male offspring. Lamentably, these young men were not only rebellious but were "the very vilest of sinners." (Mosiah 27:10; 28:4.)

It is difficult to visualize how Mosiah coped with the immense grief and humiliation his sons' actions must have caused him. And yet, with what could be considered by some as failure at home, we know Mosiah was a righteous king, a valiant steward, a man of God, and a seer. He remained faithful and strong and did not become debilitated by what must have been a great personal sorrow.

> Sometimes the most challenging form of endurance is found in trying to stay with our priorities, commitments, and assignments. How easy it is for some of us to lose our way when the unexpected, and seemingly undeserved, surface in our lives. Greatness is best measured by how well an individual responds to the happenings in life that appear to be totally unfair, unreasonable, and undeserved. Sometimes we are inclined to put up with a situation rather than endure. To endure is to bear up under, to stand firm against, to suffer without yielding, to continue to be, or to exhibit the state or power of lasting. . . . Sometimes our cross, as we carry it, gives us a new outlook and a new eternal dimension. (Marvin J. Ashton, *Be of Good Cheer* [Salt Lake City: Deseret Book Co., 1987], pp. 21–22, 99.)

Alma the Younger: Bitter and Sweet

Alma the Elder was a priest in the court of wicked King Noah. The Lord sent the prophet Abinadi to call King Noah and his people to repentance. Alma listened, repented, and after the death of Abinadi became the leader of the Church in his area.

After Alma and his band of Christian followers had to flee the city to elude the savage King Noah they were placed under bondage by the Lamanites. Alma's group exercised faith, trusted in the Lord, and were obedient during their trials, and eventually they were able to escape from the Lamanites and find their way to Zarahemla. King Mosiah openly welcomed the refugees and gladly absorbed them into his kingdom. Alma was eventually appointed high priest of the land. He taught the gospel of Christ, organized the true church, and led with justice and mercy.

Studying the lives of Alma the Elder and Alma the Younger can teach us many important lessons. Parents can learn to stop reproaching themselves for their own past transgressions. In our struggles to find answers to the madness that surrounds us we often allow ourselves to be "harrowed up" by our past and we re-condemn ourselves needlessly for long-ago-forgiven sins. The Lord forgets our sins when we sincerely repent (see D&C 58:42); it is unnecessary to continually bring them to mind.

In addition the second article of faith states: "We believe that men will be punished for their own sins, and not for Adam's transgression." Just as we are not punished for Adam's transgression, our children are not punished for ours, and vice versa. "The son shall not bear the iniquity of the father, neither shall the father bear the iniquity of the son" (Ezekiel 18:20). The scriptures clarify that we each have our agency and are judged in accordance with our knowledge and light.

The story of Alma the Younger is a striking example of re-pentance: a rebellious son, sorrowing parents, supportive friends, self-realization, the "bitter pain and anguish of . . . soul," angelic intervention, redemption from "the pains of hell" through the marvelous atonement, and spiritual cleansing. "And oh, what joy, and what marvelous light I did behold; yea my soul was filled with joy as exceeding as was my pain!" (Alma 36:20.) It is essential for us to know that through repentance and the Savior's atoning sacrifice we and our loved ones can stand clean and pure before God. President Ezra Taft Benson has commented:

Because He was God—even the Son of God—He could carry the weight and burden of other men's sins on Himself. . . . That holy, unselfish act of voluntarily taking on Himself the sins of all other men is the Atonement. How One could bear the sins for all is beyond the comprehension of mortal man. But this I know: He did take on Himself the sins of all and did so out of His infinite love for each of us. (*Ensign*, April 1991, p. 2.)

Tragically, there are many Latter-day Saint prodigals who have stumbled and fallen so far that they presume they are beyond the reach of our Savior's restoring power. They listen to Satan's clever lies of hopelessness and futility. But to the contrary, the Lord has explicitly declared that they are not beyond his redeeming powers. Elder Boyd K. Packer has said:

In the battle of life, the adversary takes enormous numbers of prisoners, and many who know of no way to escape and are pressed into his service. Every soul confined to a concentration camp of sin and guilt has a key to the gate. The adversary cannot hold them if they know how to use it. The key is labeled *Repentance*. The twin principles of repentance and forgiveness exceed in strength the awesome power of the adversary.

I know of no sins connected with the moral standard for which we cannot be forgiven. I do not exempt abortion. The formula is stated in forty words:

"Behold, he who has repented of his sins, the same is forgiven, and I, the Lord, remember them no more. By this ye may know if a man repenteth of his sins—behold, he will confess them and forsake them." (D&C 58:42–43.) (*Ensign*, May 1992, p. 68.)

When we realize that God's mercy, love, and power are stronger than the adversary's cunning, we know (exercising faith and hope) that our battle-worn children can choose to return so that the light of redeeming hope and grace will shine again in their lives. For Christ came "to give light to them that sit in darkness" (Luke 1:79).

Alma the Younger, the four sons of Mosiah, Paul, and the people of Ammon unitedly bear witness that God truly remembers our sins no more and that once-defiant souls can become great laborers in his kingdom. What sweet comfort it is to parents of a prodigal to know that the Lord is the "same God yesterday, today, and forever" (D&C 20:12). There is always hope in Christ.

Adam and Eve: A Shadow of Things to Come

Adam and Eve are two parents who endured what surely must be the worst trial a parent can undergo—to have one son murder another. If ever any two suffered the agonies of parenthood, it must be Adam and Eve, our courageous ancestors. There was no blame on their head; Adam and Eve did what the Lord required them to do: "And Adam and Eve blessed the name of God, and they made all things known unto their sons and their daughters." Cain exercised his agency: "behold, Cain hearkened not." The Lord himself spoke to Cain and explained the consequences of his choice, but "Cain loved Satan more than God." (Moses 5:12, 16, 18.)

Cain was taught correct principles by his parents and by the Lord, but he deliberately turned away from their guidance to follow Satan's path to destruction. What a horrible feeling of failure this could have evoked in his parents. It was not Adam and Eve, however, but their rebellious son Cain who let his selfish greed, personal ambition, and spiteful envy hinder his progress.

> There is no man in this Church and kingdom, and certainly no woman, who does not feel a sense of failure more or less often. . . . Children fail to take the counsel of their parents and parents grieve bitterly, both because of sorrow at the child's wrongdoing and because of the implied failure in the training of the parents. No one who has neither son nor daughter can measure the despair

of the father or mother who is powerless to prevent the loved child from taking a downward course, and yet each child is as much a son and daughter of God as we ourselves are. . . .

Let us, once and for all, accept the thought that we must be succored in affliction and tested by temptation and seeming failure ere we have either wisdom or strength to climb the upward path toward heaven and salvation. . . .

No man or woman is, or can possibly be, a failure who has striven to do good and struggled to overcome individual temptation. . . . No woman [or man] . . . is a failure because she . . . has had . . . children turn away from the truth. Failures in life are those who permit selfish greed, personal ambition, or spiteful envy . . . to prevent personal progress and personal development. . . . Let us thank the Lord that the gospel is a gospel of hope, not despair—of constant repentance and regeneration, not final, or eternal, punishment. (*Relief Society Magazine*, February 1921, pp. 111–12.)

Elder Howard W. Hunter expressed concern for the parents who define themselves as failures because they have recalcitrant children:

A successful parent is one who has loved, one who has sacrificed, and one who has cared for, taught, and ministered to the needs of a child. If you have done all of these and your child is still wayward or troublesome or worldly, it could well be that you are, nevertheless, a successful parent. Perhaps there are children who have come into the world that would challenge any set of parents under any set of circumstances. Likewise, perhaps there are others who would bless the lives of, and be a joy to, almost any father or mother. My concern today is that there are parents who may be pronouncing harsh judgments upon themselves and may be allowing these feelings to destroy their lives, when in fact they have done their best and should continue in faith. (*Ensign*, November 1983, p. 65.)

In Moses 5:27 we observe the depth of sorrow and despair that can come to all the parents of defiant children: "Adam and his wife mourned before the Lord, because of Cain and his brethren." This was a foreshadowing of things yet to come; just as the first father and mother mourned over the choices their son made, so would their descendants Isaac and Rebekah mourn over Esau. Jacob mourned over Reuben, Levi, and Simeon. Presumably Judah mourned over Er. The prophet Samuel likely mourned over his sons Joel and Abiah. Lehi and Sariah grieved over their rebellious sons. Mosiah suffered over his four sons. Alma the Elder and Alma the Younger grieved over their wayward ones; so also would many future exemplary parents "mourn before the Lord" over the choices made by their offspring. You who are the father or mother of a rebellious and reckless child share in common the experience of some of God's choicest servants.

What Could I Have Done More?

Moses briefly recorded the Lord's account of the Council in Heaven and Lucifer's resulting rebellion. The Doctrine and Covenants also gives us a glimpse of the loss suffered by the celestial parents of this son of the morning:

> And this we saw also, and bear record, that an angel of God who was in authority in the presence of God, who rebelled against the Only Begotten Son whom the Father loved and who was in the bosom of the Father, was thrust down from the presence of God and the Son, and was called Perdition, for the heavens wept over him—he was Lucifer, a son of the morning. And we beheld, and lo, he is fallen! is fallen, even a son of the morning! (D&C 76:25–27.)

God has surely suffered more than we can understand with our limited capacities. "The loss of a soul is a very real and a very great loss to God. He is pained and grieved thereby, for it is His will that not one should perish." (James E. Talmage, *Jesus the*

Christ [Salt Lake City: The Church of Jesus Christ of Latter-day Saints, 1962], p. 461.) He lost a third part of his offspring following the War in Heaven. He was the perfect parent. We in our grief can confidently turn to Heavenly Father for solace, empathy, and inspiration.

> To whom do we look, in days of grief and disaster, for help and consolation? . . . Men and women who have suffered, and out of their experience in suffering . . . bring forth the riches of their sympathy and condolences as a blessing to those now in need. Could they do this had they not suffered themselves? . . .
>
> Is not this God's purpose in causing his children to suffer? He wants them to become more like himself. God has suffered far more than man ever did or ever will, and is therefore the great source of sympathy and consolation. (Orson F. Whitney, *Improvement Era*, November 1918, p. 7.)

A reassuring story for any grieving parent is the allegory of the olive tree, found in the fifth chapter of Jacob. This relates to God's dealings with his children; more specifically, with his chosen or covenant children, Israel. And we can perhaps see in it parallels to our dealings with *our* children. It may be we can learn how to cope as we see that the Lord of the vineyard (Jesus Christ) is continually employing alternative strategies in managing his vineyard. (In the following paragraph the words in parentheses are intended not as interpretations of the scripture but as indications—sometimes suggesting parallels—of how parents might creatively foster and care for their own "olive tree"—their children.)

Utilizing the help of his servants or prophets—those with stewardship—the master of the vineyard plucks off branches (suggests weaknesses to be worked on) and grafts on wild branches (provides unlikely and varied experiences); digs or weeds about the plants (nourishes them with scriptures and prophets); transplants to alternate locations (puts them in the right environment); and dungs the soil (works us through our afflictions). He uses every means at his disposal to grow the trees to the point at which they will produce good fruit (obedient behavior). But despite all he does, some parts of the tree (his children) bring forth bad fruit (prodigal behavior).

In a revealing verse we can see plainly the Lord's sense of loss and frustration: "And it came to pass that the Lord of the vineyard wept, and said unto the servant: What could I have done more for my vineyard? . . . Have I slackened mine hand, that I have not nourished it? Nay, I have nourished it, and I have digged about it, and I have pruned it, and I have dunged it; and I have stretched forth mine hand almost all the day long, and the end draweth nigh. And it grieveth me." (Jacob 5:41, 47.)

Haven't we ourselves also said at some time: What more could I have done with my children? Haven't I said prayers with them, read the scriptures with them, held family home evening, taken them to church? Have I not nourished them and loved them? What more could I have done?

"There is a law, irrevocably decreed in heaven before the foundation of this world, upon which all blessings are predicated—and when we obtain any blessing from God, it is by obedience to that law upon which it is predicated" (D&C 130:20–21). All the commandments have blessings attached. The blessings are there for our children if they want them. Our job is to teach correct principles. Their job is to grasp them. If you have done your job, even imperfectly, prayerfully evaluate, move forward, and stop beating yourself!

Elder James E. Faust has spoken of children's agency:

> Children are also beneficiaries of moral agency by which we are all afforded the opportunity to progress, grow, and develop. That agency also permits children to pursue the alternate choice of selfishness, wastefulness, self-indulgence, and self-destruction. Children often express this agency when very young.
>
> Let parents who have been conscientious, loving, and concerned and who have lived the principles of righteousness as best they could be comforted in knowing that they are good parents

despite the actions of some of their children. The children themselves have a responsibility to listen, obey, and, having been
taught, to learn. Parents cannot always answer for all their children's misconduct because they cannot ensure the children's
good behavior. Some few children could tax even Solomon's wisdom and Job's patience. (*Ensign*, November 1990, p. 34.)

As this chapter has discussed, certain concepts will help
protect us from being pulled down by guilt and shame when
children turn wayward:

1. Feelings of guilt arising from the waywardness of one's
   child do not emanate from our Father in Heaven.
2. Father in Heaven is aware of your struggle; he loves you
   and values you for your righteous endeavors.
3. You must maintain your own spiritual integrity, particularly during this difficult time.
4. Children have agency and will use it.
5. Your job is to teach the correct principles. Your child's
   job is to grasp them.
6. If you have done your job, even imperfectly, stop beating
   yourself.

2

Be Still and Know
that I Am God

Our Father in Heaven has perfect love for his children. A great example of this love is found in the gift of his Only Begotten Son, Jesus Christ. Gethsemane is our paradigm for all suffering, anguish, sorrow, and burdens as we see that great suffering was needed in order to bring great good. At some moment in his acute agony in Gethsemane, Jesus called out to his Father, "Abba, Father, all things are possible to thee" (Mark 14:36). The LDS Bible Dictionary tells us that *Abba* is a personal and familial term for *father*. Paul extends our personal family linkage to the Father when he asserts: "For as many as are led by the Spirit of God, they are the sons of God. . . . Whereby we cry, Abba, Father." (Romans 8:14–15.)

Many hundreds of years later, Joseph Smith corroborated the divine linkage and amplified the concept as the foundation of the restored gospel: "It is the first principle of the gospel to know for a certainty the character of God, and to know that we may converse with Him as one man converses with another" (*History of the Church* 6:305). Our Father is always accessible and willing to listen, guide, and comfort. He waits for us. And though our suffering at worst is much less than the anguish of the Savior's atonement, our prayers for help also bring the attention and compassion of a loving Father who knows us by name and our problems in detail. "How glorious it is to address such a holy and exalted person by the greatest of all titles, Father, and to be privileged to have audience with him on our own invitation, anytime we pray in faith with all the strength and energy of our souls!" (Bruce R. McConkie, *The Mortal Messiah*, 4 vols. [Salt Lake City: Deseret Book Co., 1979–81], 2:15.)

To know that the God who created the measureless heaven and earth is an intimate guardian of each of us is a profound comfort. What a peace-rendering gift are his words, "Be still and know that I am God" (D&C 101:16).

I Will Give You Rest

Moments may occur when we are so debilitated by grief that our Father in Heaven intervenes. Uniquely, he is "a refuge from the storm" (Isaiah 25:4). He is a safe harbor, our haven of peace and our shelter of love. We pray to the Father who is omniscient and omnipotent. We read in Alma 7:11 that through the Atonement Jesus personally knows and understands not only our anguish resulting from sin but also our pains and afflictions. The third member of the Godhead, the Holy Ghost, is also known as the Comforter. A scriptural name and title is furnished to symbolize his intimate mission to us, individually and collectively (see *Teachings of the Prophet Joseph Smith*, sel. Joseph Fielding Smith [Salt Lake City: Deseret Book Co., 1938], p. 150). The Father measures out blessings according to our faith, needs, and circumstances through Jesus Christ and by the Spirit. The Holy Ghost can bring solace, peace, hope, and perfect love. (See Moroni 8:26.)

Many of the following true stories (in italics) are brief snapshots that emphasize particular principles. Regrettably many details have had to be omitted from the stories that would otherwise more explicitly convey the time, effort, and agony entailed in the process of a parent's gaining peace or the prodigal's returning. These stories are intended to share hope, to show the

Lord's love, and to demonstrate that he answers prayers. We must have faith in the answers we receive and must wait upon the Lord's timetable.

> *He was such a gentle, kind boy. It was hard to believe he had done such a senseless thing. But he had, and he was going to pay a terrible price for it. He had always been a joy and mainstay to me, so I was unable to completely comprehend this trouble he was in—I collapsed emotionally. I couldn't eat or sleep; my mind refused to function except to worry and grieve.*
>
> *Thankfully, there was solace for my pain. Whenever the suffering became too great to bear, I would go to my Father in Heaven in desperate prayer, not really even knowing what to say. Even now it's hard to explain. I only know that I felt as if I were placing my head on his heavenly lap and that somehow he put his loving arms around me. Somehow my desperate agony was bearable because he loved me so. But, just as with the manna sent from heaven to the Israelites crossing the desert, this gracious outpouring was there only so long as I was in desperate need. My Heavenly Father knew when I had gained strength from him enough to bear my sorrows with less help from him.*

When we turn to the Lord in sincere, humble prayer, he will be there for us. We never need to worry that our prayers will be considered unimportant to him. "For your Father knoweth what things ye have need of before ye ask him" (3 Nephi 13:8). One of the great blessings we have is to know he is personally at hand. President N. Eldon Tanner said: "I often wonder if we really realize the power of prayer, if we appreciate what a great blessing it is to be able to call on our Father in heaven in humble prayer, knowing that he is interested in us and that he wants us to succeed" (in *Prayer* [Salt Lake City: Deseret Book Co., 1977], p. 123).

> *Daybreak seemed to procrastinate its coming the night my daughter didn't come home. She was nowhere to be found. There had been no argument the day before, no great confrontation, no scene. Nothing made sense. I was in such turmoil that I couldn't think. What had I*

done that she should treat me so? What was I going to do to bring her home? How were we going to find her? Was she all right? She couldn't have had more than a few dollars when she left home. Where was she?

This went on for hours. I had younger children at home who also needed attention, so I tried to pull myself together. The burden was almost too much to bear. Amidst all this, I had to teach a Relief Society lesson the next day, and of all things the lesson was "A Cheerful Heart." At the time I couldn't even imagine being cheerful. I went to my closet and poured out my heart in prayer. I laid all my troubles on the Lord. Peace did not come immediately, but as the day went on I could feel his peace and comfort overtaking me. I was blessed with a special confidence that I would be able to teach the lesson and that I would be able to cope with the problems at hand. And I did.

Alone, none of us can fully meet the requirements of modern life while burdened with grief and mourning for our lost sons and daughters. The Comforter, however, can reach down and pull us out of the chasm of hopelessness and put our feet back on the sure path. God has promised, "they that mourn . . . shall be comforted" (Matthew 5:4).

Our eldest son had reached missionary age but it was a bitter time for us instead of one of sweet fulfillment because he had no intention of serving a mission. In fact, he wanted nothing to do with the Church, or with us.

My husband and I happened to be attending a temple wedding and were asked to wait in the chapel for a moment. Sitting in front of us was a young man and his mother; her arm was around him. The boy was obviously there to receive his endowment before entering the mission field. My heart ached as the picture of my son's unfulfilled potential swept over me. I poured out my heart in silent prayer. Immediately the comfort and assurance came that I would yet have sons to sit with in the temple. So far I have sat with three, including the eldest.

Heavenly Father, who knows the depths of our souls, knows when we have truly endured all that we can endure for the moment. At that pivotal juncture he can extend his comfort. Our

Savior, Jesus Christ, literally knows the breadth and depth of our pain. For this purpose he came into the world. "And he shall go forth, suffering pains and afflictions and temptations of every kind; and this that the word might be fulfilled which saith he will take upon him the pains and the sicknesses of his people. . . . that he may know according to the flesh how to succor his people according to their infirmities." (Alma 7:11–12.) Tenderly the Master speaks: "Come unto me, all ye that labour and are heavy leaden, and I will give you rest" (Matthew 11:28).

Many of those who endured isolation and torture in Vietnam war prisons found in prayer a solace and strength—even, sometimes, a release from pain.

> A dramatic description of surprising strength in faith came from Capt. Jeremiah A. Denton in Atlanta. He tells of escalating torture to get him to betray communication methods used among prisoners. After five days in a "torture rig," he says, he wrote something useless for his captors, "but they didn't buy it." He goes on:
>
> "They put me back in the same rig for five more days and that was the time I simply told God he would just have to take over. I had reached the end. I knew that if I had to write the next time, I would write something harmful, so I just turned myself over to him.
>
> "I have never had a prayer answered so spectacularly in my life. As soon as I got that prayer out, this mantle of comfort came over me and I couldn't feel any more pain. Even when they beat . . . me and tightened up right to the maximum, I was just as comfortable as if I were sitting in a plush auto." ("In Isolation, POWs Discovered God," *Deseret News*, April 6, 1973, p. 16A.)

The physical body can endure only so much pain without surrendering all reason. So also our emotional and spiritual self can reach a threshold of pain that may prompt us to surrender all hope and faith in our greatest source of hope, our Savior. But this is the very time when we must *cling* to that faith and hope.

It was an unbelievable time in my life. First my daughter became pregnant and had to get married. I was still grieving about her when my son got into serious trouble. I thought then that I had suffered all there was, and that surely no more pain would dare enter my life. "After all," I reasoned, "we have been promised that we will not have to deal with any more than we can bear," and I had borne so much. Then I received a call from a friend who had become aware of a serious problem with another one of my children. Her voice was filled with worry and concern for my mental state as she apprised me of the crisis.

But as she was explaining the problem, I could feel peace and serenity flushing through my being, from the top of my head down to my very toes. I, who should have been utterly shaken, was completely calm. I sensed that I was not carrying this load myself. My Lord had somehow lifted my sorrow. How? I do not know. I only know I was able to carry on and do what was necessary. I never did suffer during the whole crisis.

When God is going to grant such an experience, with a divine algorithm that calculates the incalculable he factors in the past, the present, the future, the condition of the heart, and all that is relevant to deciding the who, the when, the where, and the how. From the remarkable experience to the sublime (or even the absence of an experience), he alone will decide. We cannot dictate the timing, the methods, or the means of divine intervention. As to the manner of His response, President Marion G. Romney said: "Not every prayer brings a spectacular response, but every sincere and earnest prayer is heard and responded to by the Spirit of the Lord. The manner in which answers to prayer most frequently come was indicated by the Lord when he said: 'Did I not speak peace to your mind concerning the matter? What greater witness can you have than from God?'" [D&C 6:23]. (In *Prayer,* pp. 18–19.)

When we turn our lives over to the Lord we must accept whatever he asks as right and his timetable as perfect. To accept the Lord's timetable requires us to yield heart and mind to him. As Elder Neal A. Maxwell has expressed it:

Throughout scripture we encounter the need for us to remember that the Lord has His own timetable for unfolding things; it will not always accord with our schedules or our wants. When, in our extremities, we urgently call for a divine response, there may be, instead, a divine delay. This is not because God, at the moment, is inattentive or loves us less than perfectly. Rather, it is because we are being asked, at the moment, to endure more for the welfare of our souls. (*Meek and Lowly* [Salt Lake City: Deseret Book Co., 1987], p. 89.)

Guide Me with Thy Counsel

In the desperate search for a new strategy, a new approach, a new tactic, or a new method when it seems everything else has failed to reach our children, there is no comparison between the infinite wisdom of our Father in Heaven and the finite thinking of parents. He knows our children's hearts. He knows what will awaken them. He knows when they will best respond. He knows the words to say and the words that should not be said. He knows when we need to take action and when we need to wait with patience. These are his children first. He knows them. This is why we must put our complete trust in him rather than rely on our limited knowledge, our natural tendencies, our logic, and our motives.

> *My son went through a time when he was very angry with me and seemed to be doing many foolish things to "get even." I have always been a "doer," and patience has not been my strongest quality. Consequently, when my son became rebellious, my tendency was to ground him and lecture him so he would understand his foolishness and learn that he had a mother who was in every way wiser and more intelligent than he.*
>
> *Thank goodness for prayer and inspiration. On several occasions a very kind and loving Father let me know that I was to hold back, be patient, and wait rather than discipline. Now that some time has passed, I can see more clearly and I realize that if I had done it my way*

I would have pushed him too far. I'm grateful I listened to the counsel of the Lord and chose to do it his way.

Wisdom is the jewel purchased at the price of meekness. If we are seeking an answer we must be willing (meek) to accept the response and render our agency to the Lord. He will never ask us to do anything that will not ultimately bring us happiness and peace; for "the meek will he guide in judgment: and the meek will he teach his way" (Psalm 25:9).

> *It had not been easy raising my son. When he had grown to maturity I was still struggling with him. Every time I would explain to him where he needed to change he would blame me or refuse to listen. I remember one night when we had a fierce discussion that ended (as they always had) with his blaming me for his troubles. I went to the Lord with a very crucial prayer: What more could I do? What did the Lord want me to do? The answer was unmistakable: Do no more, and let the Lord handle it. In fact, I felt I shouldn't say anything more to my son. I was promised that if I would back off, God would take away the bitterness and the unhappiness, and I would have peace.*
>
> *It was not easy. I would conjure up lectures that I knew he needed to hear and I would have to bite my tongue not to speak. But in time I noticed that peace did come to me and I also saw that my son was beginning to respond.*

My Rock and My Fortress

Defiant children seem to elicit an almost universal reaction in Latter-day Saint parents: we begin to question our abilities; we wonder if we are really able to receive answers to prayer; we wonder if the Lord is listening; we anguish; we panic; we overreact; and we become frightened. Peril exists in these natural responses, because when doubt and uncertainty enter our minds faith leaves: then we are truly alone. The Prophet Joseph Smith explained the relationship between doubt and faith:

Doubt and faith do not exist in the same person at the same time; so that persons whose minds are under doubts and fears cannot have unshaken confidence; and where unshaken confidence is not there faith is weak; and where faith is weak the persons will not be able to contend against all the opposition, tribulations, and afflictions which they will have to encounter in order to be heirs of God, and joint heirs with Christ Jesus; and they will grow weary in their minds, and the adversary will have power over them and destroy them (*Lectures on Faith* 6:12).

Satan wants us to live in doubt and confusion. That's when we are powerless and he is powerful. We must develop the knowledge, skills, and abilities to subdue and conquer our emotions so we can call down the powers of heaven to sustain and guide us for the benefit of our children, our families, and ourselves. As the Psalmist found strength in the Lord so, too, can we: "I will love thee, O Lord, my strength. The Lord is my rock, and my fortress, and my deliverer; my God, my strength, in whom I will trust; my buckler, and the horn of my salvation, and my high tower. I will call upon the Lord, who is worthy to be praised: so shall I be saved from mine enemies." (Psalm 18:1–3.)

There are within our reach many sources of power and strength to which we can always turn. The Lord has sent shepherds to tend his flock. These latter-day shepherds are our priesthood leaders. The priesthood is the eternal power and authority by which all things are created, governed, and controlled. The plan of creation, redemption, and exaltation operates "worlds without number" through priesthood power. The Lord's stewards stand as his proxies to summon this power. "Whether by mine own voice or by the voice of my servants, it is the same" (D&C 1:38). The priesthood is a merciful gift to us, enabling us to receive counsel and blessings, and have, as it were, the hands of the Lord placed upon our heads and hear him speak words of comfort and enlightenment to our souls.

I was so disappointed when the arrangements fell through. I had desperately counted on moving my son out of the state—entirely away from the situation that was dragging him down. I had convinced myself that moving him away was all that it would take to make him come back to his senses.

Then the phone call came—the move was off. Now what would I do? We had tried everything. It seemed hopeless. Despair grew like a weed. I was angry at my Heavenly Father for letting me down. Even after much prayer, fasting, and time in the temple, I was still distraught.

Then a good friend felt inspired to call me. She suggested I get some counseling and a blessing from our priesthood leader. Our priesthood leader counseled my husband and me and gave us both blessings. The blessing was just what I needed to go on. A clear impression came to me that there are times when some children are so severely wounded by life that they are extremely vulnerable—like a bloody fish in shark-infested waters. In this case, moving him to new waters, as it were, would have drawn new sharks and the same problems all over again. It was then that I began to grasp that for now only repentance, forgiveness, and the Lord's timetable could heal my son's wounds. Peace returned to my soul even though the problems persisted.

Church leaders are given gifts of the Spirit and hold the keys that can unlock the doors of darkness. We need to understand that these men and women are called by God; he will inspire his servants and will let them know when hearts have been softened and lives are ready to be changed. For example, a Relief Society president found it necessary to keep a pad of paper and pencil by her bed. After finishing her nightly prayers, it was not unusual for her to feel impressed to write down a sister's name. When this occurred, she would pray again, concentrating her prayer on the specified sister, requesting further inspiration as to what she as the Relief Society president should do to fulfill her stewardship. After being released from that calling, she was able to put her pad and pencil away.

After my son Bill returned from his mission he committed a serious transgression, and because of embarrassment and other factors he be-

came inactive and alienated. *There had been much prayer and fasting by his family on his behalf. Nevertheless, he still shied away from the Church or anything to do with it.*

One day, as I was praying, I felt strongly that Bill was struggling within himself and needed help. "Perhaps," I thought, "if he had a little push from the Lord it might help." So I began to pray and fast specifically for him. Within a few days, his bishop and his stake president came to visit him. When Bill commented on the rarity of having both of them visit, he was told, "It is the practice of the stake leaders to meet periodically and go through the list of less-active members, to kneel as a group and pray about who they should visit, and to list in order of consideration five names to be visited." The first name on every leader's list that day was my son Bill. I was grateful that my prayer had been answered in a most discernible manner.

Jacob, the brother of Nephi, advised us to "take counsel from [the Lord's] hand" (Jacob 4:10). We are all unique, and the Lord knows us, loves us, and deals with us better than a human can. Because he knows our children, who they were, who they are, and what they can become, we can have confidence in the truths he will teach us about them. "One of the most difficult parental challenges" Elder James E. Faust has said, "is to appropriately discipline children. Child rearing is so individualistic. Every child is different and unique. What works with one may not work with another. . . . It is a matter of prayerful discernment for the parents." (*Ensign*, November 1990, p. 34.)

Two strong-willed children taught me how very important it is to listen to the guidance of the Spirit when raising children. Although these children appeared to have similar personalities, evidently they had very different needs that only the Lord understood. Often I felt that different, almost opposite disciplinary methods were needed for them. With the older one the Spirit would whisper, "Don't let him overpower you. He needs to learn to control his strong nature." He thanks me now for the courage he knows I displayed in disciplining him as a youngster.

Using the same methods with his younger brother, however, brought disaster. Trying harder made things even worse. Finally, I asked for heavenly guidance. (I'm sorry to say that it took reaching the end of my wits and endurance before I humbled myself sufficiently to do it.) The answer I received was quite definite: "Just love him. Let him see that you love and value him." Every time I would try to come down on him for misbehavior, the Spirit seemed to pull me back and I was prompted to show him an increase of love (instead of an increase of correction, which I felt more inclined to do). For a long time, our relationship had been less then wonderful, but when I started "just loving" him we began to become closer. He was drawn more and more to the Lord's way despite himself.

There are times when parents become so entangled in the drama of a prodigal crisis, particularly when it goes on for months or years, that they may conclude that a miraculous manifestation is the only way left to make things work out. Sometimes we forget that we are also the "child," with much to learn, develop, and endure. Again, Jacob reminds us: "Seek not to counsel the Lord, but to take counsel from his hand" (Jacob 4:10). We must be willing to bend our will to his if we want to have the Spirit of truth. If we want to receive more answers we must accept the answers we are receiving now and follow through with a proper attitude, though they seem contrary to our will or hard for us.

My son had left home and returned several times. He was sullen and abusive and most of his nastiness was directed at me. I really believe he hated me. I went to the Lord in prayer again and again. What was the answer? I asked the Lord to soften my son's heart. I asked the Lord to discipline him. I asked the Lord to show him his error. I just knew that what was really needed was an angel to appear to my ungrateful child and call him to repentance for treating me in such an awful manner.

Finally, in sheer desperation, I begged and pleaded with my Heavenly Father so that I could help myself help my son. That's when I got an answer—not by an angel to bring about his change. The answer was that I should change. More than that, I was given the very words to say to him so that he would know I had changed.

One day I went to my son's room when he was alone and asked for his forgiveness. I told him how sorry I was that I had focused on his negative traits and had overlooked what a wonderful and noble young man he was. I promised him that I would never be guilty of such behavior again.

I have kept my promise. He did not become my friend overnight; he was very wary of me. But slowly over the months and years I was able to build his trust in me. I am so happy that this wonderful young man and I are now close and becoming closer.

Revelation is any divine truth received by communication from God, and he chooses a variety of ways to communicate with his children. The Prophet Joseph Smith taught: "A person may profit by noticing the first intimation of the spirit of revelation; for instance, when you feel pure intelligence flowing into you, it may give you sudden strokes of ideas. . . . and thus by learning the Spirit of God and understanding it, you may grow into the principle of revelation." (*Teachings of the Prophet Joseph Smith*, p. 151.)

Things were rarely peaceful at home. My reaction was to rebel completely against my parents. In doing so, I made a pretty good mess of my life. This went on for a few years. However, the Lord did not let it go on too long. One day as I was in the shower, a deep impression came to my mind that I needed to begin the process of repenting so that I could straighten out my life. This feeling was followed by a spirit of assurance that the impression I had just had was true. That was the beginning of my new life. I repented, went on a mission, and a few years later married a wonderful girl in the temple. I have never looked back, but now I try to do what Heavenly Father wants.

Often we don't recognize the prompting of the Spirit because it comes quietly and perhaps unexpectedly. We may think of revelation in terms of a lofty and substantial experience, but the Lord has said, "Out of small things proceedeth that which is great" (D&C 64:33).

I have always been ashamed to show emotion, especially tears. To me it's embarrassing to cry. My two children were exceptionally close, so when the oldest son started sneaking out of the house late at night he enlisted his younger sister's help to cover for him. I knew what was going on and I had to find some way to stop this before the younger sister was dragged into this behavior also.

After praying for guidance, I talked to my daughter when she was working in the kitchen one day. I told her that, although we had not seen eye to eye on everything, I knew I could rely on her honesty. I also told her that I had always trusted her. My feelings began to well up inside me and I started to push them back as usual, but I had a strong impression to let them go—to let her see my pain. So I let go. The tears started to come out and my voice cracked, and I started to cry. I could tell that she was deeply moved. She promised me then that she would never help her brother to sneak out again. As far as I know, she kept that promise.

What about the times when the situation is so utterly desperate that there seems no way out? Heavenly Father knows the way, and prayer is the means whereby we can take his lead. We may have explored every avenue at our disposal. We may have truly met the insurmountable wall of which President David O. McKay spoke. "You will meet a wall that seems insurmountable, impregnable. . . . When you get there, and you have gone as far as you can, you will find in answer to your prayer that there is a hidden ladder by which you can scale it, or there is a door which you could not see from where you were first standing. God's hand is shown. In that hour you become responsive to the infinite." (As quoted by Elder John H. Vandenberg in *Prayer*, p. 121.)

And as we diligently, steadfastly, and humbly seek his counsel and guidance, then the promise is, "the Lord thy God shall lead thee by the hand, and give thee answers to thy prayers" (D&C 112:10).

As a lawyer I had a case in which a young man named Joe had gotten himself into serious trouble. He had been foolish and had broken the law. Because there had been so many other similar cases in our area, the police and courts decided to make an example of this young man and prosecute him to the limit. His devastated parents were close friends of mine, and I had known this boy since his childhood. I knew him to be a good boy, if a bit imprudent. This court business could ruin his life. I really worried about this case.

One day as I was out working in my yard I had a feeling come over me that I should pray, so I went to the quiet corner of my yard and did so. I asked the Lord to let me know what I should do to help this boy. A strong impression came to me that I should call the detective in charge of the case. Now I must explain that a defense lawyer simply does not associate with the arresting detective; it just isn't done. But that is exactly what I felt I should do. When I called him, he asked me to bring the boy in to see him because there were still some questions about the case.

I took Joe in to see the detective and they talked for about an hour. Later the detective told me how surprised he was with my client because he wasn't anything like he had expected. He was "a nice, clean-cut, well-spoken young man." From that time on the detective was my ally, and eventually it was his influence that helped to get Joe a sentence that was disciplinary but not devastating to his life.

With God Nothing Shall Be Impossible

There are passages in the scriptures which bring to the mind a beautiful, poetic imagery. For example: "Behold, I stand at the door, and knock: if any man hear my voice, and open the door, I will come in to him, and will sup with him, and he with me" (Revelation 3:20). In his divine humility and patience the Savior stands at our door, knocks, and calls to us. His delicate announcement that he will come to us, and that we may feast with him, enters our heart. But we must answer the door. He will invite, entice, and persuade, but we must come to him. "I know thy works: behold, I have set before thee an open door" (Revelation 3:8). Nowhere in this image is there the slightest whiff of coercion. Christ, the great High Priest, with the power of the universe awaiting his command, is in flawless control. "The power of the Priesthood is to be exercised in the spirit of patience and love, and not in opposition to individual free agency" (James E. Talmage, *Articles of Faith* [Salt Lake City: The Church of Jesus Christ of Latter-day Saints, 1966], p. 493).

Elder Howard W. Hunter has observed:

> To fully understand this gift of agency and its inestimable worth, it is imperative that we understand that God's chief way of acting is by persuasion and patience and long-suffering, not by coercion and stark confrontation. He acts by gentle solicitation and sweet enticement. He always acts with unfailing respect for the freedom and independence that we possess. He wants to help us and pleads for the chance to assist us, but he will not do so in violation of our agency. He loves us too much to do that, and doing so would run counter to his divine character. (*Ensign*, November 1989, p. 18.)

We must be free in this life to choose the Lord's way or the world's way. The Lord will do everything possible, except usurp agency, to bring a person back into his confidence. We must do likewise in order to enjoy the supportive powers of heaven. Our training skills, disciplinary practices, and coaching techniques must also reflect these precepts. Experience shows, however, that one of the greatest challenges for parents with prodigals is managing the inevitable tension between agency and intervention. The Lord has given us guidance that power or influence over others can legitimately be used "only by persuasion, by long-suffering, by gentleness and meekness, and by love unfeigned; by kindness, and pure knowledge . . . without hypocrisy, and without guile" (D&C 121:41–42).

An example of this dilemma comes from the authors' own family. Mother was promised in her patriarchal blessing that our father would join the Church. The fulfillment of that prophecy took twenty-seven demanding, perplexing, and arduous years. Father was hard-hearted and embittered against the Church.

The word *Mormon* never stood alone in Father's vocabulary— he always preceded it with a negative adjective. He even collected articles so that for his children he could write a book against the Church.

When Father was seventy years old he had a heart attack and needed surgery. After his surgery he had to spend two weeks flat on his back in the hospital. In the long, quiet nights he began to question his life and realized that, while he was loved by his children, there was some evidence that they didn't like him. For the next eight years Father worked on repairing and rebuilding a relationship with his family. We could see his heart slowly soften, and his will align with the Lord's.

When Father was seventy-eight years old, he agreed to read the Book of Mormon. The Lord seemed to use every approach, method, and strategy in his divine repertoire to tutor Father: family, friends, Church leaders, the priesthood, spiritual promptings, prayer and fasting, studying, searching, and pondering. Finally the incredible happened—he joined the Church. Indeed, "With God nothing shall be impossible" (Luke 1:37).

During the many years of Father's conversion, our family was blessed to experience many incidents of divine direction concerning him. Most of these came in the form of sweet impressions, not obviously miraculous events. Yet we had often wished for a great miracle to change his heart. We knew of spectacular conversions in the scriptures, such as Alma's and Paul's (see Mosiah 27; Acts 9). We wrestled with what seemed to be the perplexing balance between agency and signs. We questioned the depth of our faith and at times even felt guilty because we were "not worthy" enough to call down the same kind of miracle from heaven. But, oh, the wisdom of the Lord! For not only did Father's heart eventually change, but also our understanding of these principles changed. The long season of his conversion converted us.

President Spencer W. Kimball's words at the Munich Germany Area Conference in 1973 convey well the slow and steady method of guidance the Lord usually employs.

The burning bushes, the smoking mountains, . . . the Cumorahs and the Kirtlands were realities; but they were the exceptions. The great volume of revelation came to Moses and to Joseph and comes to today's prophet in the less spectacular way—that of deep impressions, without spectacle or glamour or dramatic events. Always expecting the spectacular, many will miss entirely the constant flow of revealed communication. (As quoted by Elder Graham W. Doxey, *Ensign*, November 1991, p. 25.)

Time is one of God's greatest tools. He works subtly, and patiently. God has all the patience we lack. Many of his works may go unnoticed by us unless we remember that "every thing which inviteth to do good, and to persuade to believe in Christ, is sent forth by the power and gift of Christ; wherefore ye may know with a perfect knowledge it is of God" (Moroni 7:16).

In time, a grotesque larva becomes a brilliant butterfly, a drab rock is split open to reveal exquisite crystals, purple hair becomes a short cut in a dark suit, and baton-twirling teenyboppers become valiant mothers in Zion. We look at our neighbors and say, "When did that happen?" not realizing the hours of prayer that parents and family have spent in a child's behalf.

> *A boy in our ward who thought he was unappreciated at home decided to join a band and become a rock singer. For a long time we did not really hear of him except that he was away "doing his own thing." Then, with no fuss or fanfare, he moved back home. His hair was long and he looked a mess, but he was back home.*
>
> *Before long he started to come to church with his parents. A little later the bishop called him to a Church position. By then he was pulling his hair back into a pony tail. After a while he cut his hair to shoulder length; then he cut it to the nape of the neck. Pretty soon it was cut in a missionary style. Two weeks later he received his mission call.*

The Lord often allows us, the every-day members of the Church, to be instruments in his hands. He gives each of us in our small fishbowl the opportunity to lift and serve others.

Jim wore his hair long and never missed a hard rock concert. Rarely could he go a day without seeking an artificial high; he was loose and promiscuous; he was failing every class in school (partly because he rarely attended); and he was in constant trouble with the law. His father and mother cried continually to the Lord for Jim to return to the Church.

One day, while making a rare appearance in the hallways of the high school, Jim saw Lisa and asked her out. She replied, "Jim, until you change your life and begin honoring your priesthood, I won't go out with you."

No girl had said that to him before. It shocked him into taking a serious look at his life. Remembering the words of his parents and his seminary teacher, he visited his bishop and began the long process of repentance. He cut his hair, and obeyed the Word of Wisdom and the law of chastity. He finally blessed the sacrament, and was ordained an Elder. (And, yes, my sister Lisa went out with him.)

"God does notice us, and he watches over us. But it is usually through another mortal that he meets our needs." (Spencer W. Kimball, *The Teachings of Spencer W. Kimball* [Salt Lake City: Bookcraft, 1982], p. 252.) We may not recognize the light that emanates from us, and we may not realize that gospel precepts are integrated into the fiber of our characters, but others do. Because of that, the Lord can use us. Perhaps when Ralph W. Emerson said, "If you would lift me, you must be on higher ground" he didn't mean we have to be standing on a mountaintop—a small mound will do.

The reason why I stand at this podium at my missionary farewell today is my friend George. I had been questioning my testimony, my parents, and my leaders, and basically had decided not to go on a mission. I told all this to George. He told me that the Church was true, and that if I had any doubt of it I was to get on my knees until I regained my testimony. Then he really got tough with me by saying, "If you want me for a friend you had better go on a mission." I guess you can see that I value George highly as a friend and I didn't want to lose him. I followed his advice and found myself at the bishop's office filling out my missionary application.

Almost everyone has had an experience in life in which a
stranger had a major influence on them. Those who have quietly and faithfully followed the admonition of Christ, "Let your
light so shine before men, that they may see your good works,
and glorify your Father which is in heaven" (Matthew 5:16)
have touched many lives.

Darla Hanks has written about letting our lights shine.

Sister Lawson's day had been a long and busy one filled with
lectures, travel, and details. In the evening she gave a special talk
on morality to the young women of the Long Beach Stake. There
was one girl in particular, Joyce, who was deeply moved and
troubled by the message.

After the meeting, Sister Lawson was surrounded by young
women wishing to speak with her. Joyce sat alone, hesitant to
join the others, yet reluctant to leave. She waited unnoticed on
the back row as the others left.

It was late. Sister Lawson was tired and anxious to get home
to her own family, and she had a long drive ahead of her. The
stake leaders were turning off the lights and locking up the building. Joyce was nervously indecisive, and started to leave several
times while Sister Lawson was gathering up her things. Then she
turned quickly and with an urgent tone in her voice asked,
"Please, Sister Lawson, may I talk to you?" Sister Lawson forgot
how tired she was, took Joyce by the arm, and they went and sat
on the front steps of the building and watched the last of the
leaders leave. Then Joyce told her story. She was on the verge of
making a serious mistake that could have had the effect of mar-
ring her life permanently. Sister Lawson's counsel and help pre-
vented that mistake from happening.

Joyce lived fifty miles in the opposite direction from Sister
Lawson's home, so she had to drive an extra hundred miles out of
her way to take Joyce home that night. She made use of every
mile to listen to Joyce's feelings, express her own empathy, and to
kindly impress Joyce with the seriousness of what she had been
about to do. When Joyce got out of the car, she promised Sister
Lawson that she would tell her parents about her problem, and

that she would never put herself in that kind of predicament again.

A few years later, while attending a session in the Los Angeles Temple, Sister Lawson was surprised when a radiant bride ran up and threw her arms around her. "You don't remember me, do you?" the bride queried. "I'm Joyce, the girl you saved from making a serious mistake five years ago in Garden Grove. Sister Lawson, it's because you took the time to listen to me and to help me that night that I am here to get married the right way." (*Ensign*, April 1979, p. 16.)

At times, adversity can prove to be a more effective minister for good than anything else. There are times when shameful and horrifying situations will cause young people to awaken and look at what they have reduced their lives to. Suffering can be the rudder that turns them around and brings them back to the Lord's harbor. From the parents' point of view, however, observing a child's suffering without overtly intervening may be the hardest thing they have to endure.

You could say that I was a really bad kid. My problem was cocaine. I was hooked and would do just about anything to take care of my habit. My parents had tried just about everything (even rehabilitation programs), but nothing worked.

One night when I was at a booze and drug party, we got busted. Since I was obviously under the influence, I was arrested. My parents hired a lawyer, but I was sent to jail anyway. I was never so scared of anything in my life. I wanted out of there in the worst way. As a last resort I even tried praying. I promised the Lord I would do anything if he would get me out of there.

To get away from the misery of that place, I tried reading the Book of Mormon. I had never been interested in it before, but suddenly, as I read, I knew that this book was the word of God. There and then, in that horrible place, I gained a testimony. I was in jail for a little over three months. I know that the Lord kept me in there until I had read the Book of Mormon because as soon as I had read it, they let me out. I went on to serve a full-time mission.

The pain, sorrow, and suffering involved in the process of repentance will be related to the degree of the sin. Our hope in Christ is the catalyst for repentance. "Hope is indeed the great incentive to repentance, for without it no one would make the difficult, extended effort required—especially when the sin is a major one" (Spencer W. Kimball, *The Miracle of Forgiveness* [Salt Lake City: Bookcraft, 1969], p. 340).

The consequences of sin can be compared to the predicament of extracting a fishhook from a thumb. If the hook has only punctured the surface skin it can be pulled out without much pain or skin damage, and healing will take place quickly. Because of the sharp barbs on the hook, however, the deeper it is imbedded, the greater the damage to the flesh when it is extracted by pulling. There is a point at which the hook can be buried so deeply that it is more merciful to cut off the eyelet and push the hook all the way through and out the other side. Although momentarily more painful, this does less damage to the flesh than pulling the hook out, and there are considerably better prospects for good healing.

Likewise, when sins are deep and pervasive the Lord may mercifully cut off the blessings of Church membership in order to help the transgressor to full repentance. This process is initiated through a church disciplinary council. Unquestionably it is painful, but it offers unlimited hope and complete healing. There is always hope through the atonement of Christ.

My son had every opportunity that the gospel could give him, but for some reason he felt that rules never applied to him. He began to stray during his teens and his sins spiraled downward for years until his nature was thoroughly worldly.

In his mid-twenties he began to comprehend how destructive his life-style was and began to take responsibility for his actions. It was at this time that he met and wanted to marry a nice young lady. He realized he needed to change and clear up his past. When he finally went to the bishop, he held nothing back. Although he met privately with the bishop, he asked his mother and me to be with him when the stake presidency and high council presented their findings.

> *Even after all these years, I can remember the love and concern that was in that room when my son was excommunicated. The Spirit of the Lord was so strong that we could not withhold our deepest feelings from being expressed. Through the Spirit we understood that finally our son would be able to sever himself from the past and begin the process of coming back to the Lord and fulfilling his noble heritage. We are so grateful that because of the Atonement our son is not spiritually limited. How great is the mercy and love of God.*

Every time a son or daughter comes back a miracle has taken place. Some miracles are so quiet that they go unnoticed. In fact, most miracles seem to occur that way. Perhaps we like to hear about the more spectacular miracles because we hope for something similar for our children. We need to be careful in that hope, since we may not understand the preparation that has taken place prior to someone else's spectacular event. For example, when we read the story of Paul in the ninth chapter of Acts we marvel at the miracle. At first reflection it would appear that Christ comes and calls Paul, the persecutor of Saints, to repentance and Paul becomes the great defender of the Lord and a zealous apostle.

When we look a little closer, we see the Lord saying "I am Jesus whom thou persecutest: it is hard for thee to kick against the pricks" (Acts 9:5). During this week-long journey to Damascus, perhaps Paul's conscience had been working on him as he reflected on the numerous Christians he had dragged from their homes and families to be thrown into prison—a work he expected soon to duplicate in Damascus (see David O. McKay, *Ancient Apostles* [Salt Lake City: Deseret Sunday School Union, 1918], pp. 140–41). In that case, by still continuing on his present course he would be kicking against the remonstrances of his heart and his better self. But when Paul said, "What wilt thou have me do?" he showed his absolute obedience to the Lord (Acts 9:6). In contrast, the hearts of Laman and Lemuel were so hard that even the appearance of an angel and hearing the Lord's voice could not change them (see 1 Nephi 3:29; 16:39; 17:45). The Lord knows the hearts of us all. We are not qualified to judge the methods he chooses to tutor us, for he is "the Lord your God, even Jesus Christ your advocate, who knoweth the weakness of man and how to succor them who are tempted" (D&C 62:1).

My granddaughter had been the sweetest, most guileless child, so it was especially painful to watch her begin to rebel. When she started to experiment with drugs, I was absolutely beside myself, not knowing what to do to help her. I had no one else to turn to but the Lord, because her parents were in no condition to assist. My only real refuge was prayer; I spent a lot of time on my knees.

One terrible night I was called to the hospital because she had overdosed and nearly lost her life. She looked awful. Her words to me showed just how low she had sunk. "I'm sorry I lived through this," she said, "because I don't really see what I have to live for." I reassured her that I loved her very much and that God loved her and wanted her to get well. Then she said, "If God loved me, he would show me a sign."

I began, right then, to pray with all my heart that Heavenly Father would reach her somehow. The next time I went to the temple I put her name in the prayer roll along with a note, "Heavenly Father, find a way to reach my girl."

A few days later, my granddaughter was walking with a friend along a street. Walking just ahead of them were two women in deep discussion. All at once, one of the women turned quickly, walked back to the girls, raised her hand, and looking at my granddaughter said, "Stop! God wants you to live! He has much in store for you." Then the woman turned around suddenly and went on her way. My girl knew then that her Heavenly Father cared. It was just what she needed.

The Lord is aware of what it will take to bring his son or daughter to repentance. For some it may be a quiet, piercing impression. For others, like the young women in the previous account and in the one that now follows, he may use more direct and forceful means.

I received my patriarchal blessing when I was sixteen years old. Three years later I began a lengthy relationship with a young man who was not a member of the Church. I was very much in love, but there appeared to be no chance that he would join the Church. In fact, he wanted me to join his.

I happened to go to a fireside where our stake patriarch was to speak. At the last minute he became ill, so the neighboring stake's patriarch spoke in his place. As I was walking out of the chapel after his talk, he came up to me and shook my hand. Then he looked me straight in the eye and said, "You are not living up to the blessings the Lord has promised you." As he said this to me the Spirit bore a strong witness that eternity hung in the balance and I could have the blessings I had been promised or I could choose my own course.

As hard as it was to do it, I broke up with the young man. After completing a mission filled with choice experiences, I married in the temple.

We must never let ourselves lose sight of this significant fact: God is omniscient. He "knoweth all things, for all things are present before [his] eyes" (D&C 38:2). He is also completely accessible: "I have set before thee an open door" (Revelation 3:8). We need not suffer alone, because the Lord has "suffered these things for all" (D&C 19:16). He is there and he knows exactly what to do. We have only to turn to him. He has issued the invitation, "Come unto me, all ye that labour and are heavy laden, and I will give you rest" (Matthew 11:28). His invitation excludes no one.

"Take my yoke upon you . . . and ye shall find rest unto your souls" (Matthew 11:29). The dictionary indicates that a yoke is a wooden framework fastened over the necks of two animals to join them together. The Savior compared gospel principles to familiar, tangible things in order to help the Saints clearly understand his teachings. It was a very common sight in that day to see a farmer using a yoke to harness and join together two animals for the purpose of carrying a heavy load. We are being invited to "yoke" ourselves together with our Savior. He is inviting us to bind ourselves to him so that he can help us carry our load. Even though it is our burden, he is willing to carry a large portion of it. He has said, "My grace is sufficient for the meek" (Ether 12:26). We need to yoke ourselves to him and allow ourselves to be guided, strengthened, and lifted by him.

Elder Boyd K. Packer has pointed out:

If you are helpless, he is not.
If you are lost, he is not.
If you don't know what to do next, he knows.
It would take a miracle, you say?
Well, if it takes a miracle, why not?
(*Improvement Era*, December 1970, p. 107.)

3

The Whole Armor

Most parents with problem children easily identify with the analogy of a "battle" in the home—it *is* a battle. Pushing beyond the crisis of the moment, however, Elder Bruce R. McConkie reminds us that we have been engaged in another battle for as long as we can remember, and longer: "Our mortal probation is a war, a continuation of the war in heaven (Revelation 12:7–17), a war against the world, against evil, against Satan. And there are no neutrals; all men are for the Lord or they are against him." We are on the Lord's side and have covenanted to carry his banner. "The only way for the Christian soldiers to come off victorious is to put on the whole armor of God." (*Doctrinal New Testament Commentary*, 3 vols. [Salt Lake City: Bookcraft, 1965–73], 2:524.)

> Put on the whole armour of God, that ye may be able to stand against the wiles of the devil.
>
> For we wrestle not against flesh and blood, but against principalities, against powers, against the rulers of the darkness of this world, against spiritual wickedness in high places.
>
> Wherefore take unto you the whole armour of God, that ye may be able to withstand in the evil day, and having done all, to stand.

Stand therefore, having your loins girt about with truth, and having on the breastplate of righteousness;

And your feet shod with the preparation of the gospel of peace;

Above all, taking the shield of faith, wherewith ye shall be able to quench all the fiery darts of the wicked.

And take the helmet of salvation, and the sword of the Spirit, which is the word of God:

Praying always with all prayer and supplication in the Spirit, and watching thereunto with all perseverance and supplication for all saints. (Ephesians 6:11–18.)

There has never been any uncertainty as to who would be the victor. Presumably even the prince of darkness knows that the Prince of Peace will win. To the Saints in Ephesus, Paul clearly articulated the required armor and strategy for success. If we desire to stand with the victorious we must choose "this day whom [we] will serve" (Joshua 24:15) and put on the armor.

We know that this generation has been reserved for this battle—the last pivotal events before the Second Coming. President Ezra Taft Benson's words on this certainly bear repetition:

All through the ages the prophets have looked down through the corridors of time to our day. Billions of the deceased and those yet to be born have their eyes on us. Make no mistake about it—you are a marked generation. There has never been more expected of the faithful in such a short period of time. . . . Never before on the face of this earth have the forces of evil and the forces of good been as well organized. (*Speeches of the Year,* 1979, p. 59.)

The lamentable fact is that some have already been taken captive in the enemy's concentration camp and are victims of the lies and distortions of his cunning indoctrination.

Rulers of Darkness

Some years ago the garbage collectors went on strike in New York City, deserting the piles of garbage that lined every street. This created a colossal problem for the residents. The news media reported that one man found a unique way to dispose of his garbage. Every morning he took his plastic sack of garbage, put it into a box, wrapped it with beautiful paper, and put a colored bow on top. He took this package with him to the bus station. As he waited for the bus he would casually place the package on the ground beside him, then "accidentally" leave the package behind as he walked off to catch his bus. Even before he found a seat on the bus, the package would be taken. He told the newscaster that he would laugh all the way to work as he pictured someone opening the present with great anticipation only to find his garbage.

Satan's wily use of disinformation can make black look white, bitter seem sweet, and filth appear beautiful. Satan is ingenious: he wraps his garbage in a splendid box and then laughs. President Spencer W. Kimball put it in this way:

> Whoever said that sin was not fun? Whoever claimed that Lucifer was not handsome, persuasive, easy, friendly? Whoever said that sin was unattractive, undesirable, or nauseating in its acceptance?
>
> Transgression wears elegant gowns and sparkling apparel. It is highly perfumed, has attractive features, a soft voice. It is found in educated circles and sophisticated groups. It provides sweet and comfortable luxuries. Sin is easy and has a big company of bedfellows. It promises immunity from restrictions, temporary freedoms. It can momentarily satisfy hunger, thirst, desire, urges, passions, wants, without immediately paying the price. But, it begins tiny and grows to monumental proportions. It grows drop by drop, inch by inch. (*The Teachings of Spencer W. Kimball* [Salt Lake City: Bookcraft, 1982], p. 152.)

Satan may have already won a skirmish by taking a child of ours prisoner. We cannot allow ourselves, however, through the frustration of the struggle, to become so severely wounded that we too become one of his casualties. Satan is the destroyer, and all "that which is evil cometh of the devil; for the devil is an enemy unto God and fighteth against him continually" (Moroni 7:12).

Some of the weapons Satan uses against us are fear, doubt, guilt, shame, anger, bitterness, resentment, and discouragement. The time when our child is wayward is a time when we can be very vulnerable, and Satan knows it. However, "God hath not given us the spirit of fear; but of power, and of love, and of a sound mind" (2 Timothy 1:7). We must seek to love the Lord and have the Spirit with us, for "perfect love casteth out fear" (1 John 4:18).

Truth

As defined in the scriptures, truth comes from the Lord. Truth centers in God, and all his words and actions are truth. "For the word of the Lord is truth, and whatsoever is truth is light, and whatsoever is light is Spirit, even the Spirit of Jesus Christ" (D&C 84:45). Truth is an absolute. Truth never conflicts with itself; it is eternal and endures forever. "Truth is knowledge of things as they are, and as they were, and as they are to come" (D&C 93:24).

The Holy Ghost has the divine mission of giving light and truth through revelation. The Prophet Joseph Smith said: "No man can receive the Holy Ghost without receiving revelations. The Holy Ghost is a revelator." (*Teachings of the Prophet Joseph Smith*, p. 328.) All worthy men and women have the right to receive inspiration and revelation from the Lord for their own lives and their stewardships. President Joseph F. Smith taught:

> The spirit of inspiration, the gift of revelation, does not belong to one man solely; it is not a gift that pertains to the Presi-

dency of the Church and the Twelve Apostles alone. It is not confined to the presiding authorities of the Church, it belongs to every individual member of the Church; and it is the right and privilege of every man, every woman, and every child who has reached the years of accountability, to enjoy the spirit of revelation, and to be possessed of the spirit of inspiration. . . . It is the privilege of every individual member of the Church to have revelation for his own guidance, for the direction of his life and conduct. (Conference Report [hereafter referred to as CR], April 1912, p. 5.)

The Lord has blessed us with the ability to communicate with him and receive revelation from him. He always speaks clearly and distinctly, but usually he speaks these truths to us very quietly. As Elder Boyd K. Packer has explained: "The Spirit does not get our attention by shouting or shaking us with a heavy hand. Rather it whispers. It caresses so gently that if we are preoccupied we may not feel it at all. . . . Occasionally it will press just firmly enough for us to pay heed. But most of the time, if we do not heed the gentle feeling, the Spirit will withdraw and wait until we come seeking and listening." (*Ensign*, January 1983, p. 53.)

Often the Lord uses the circumstances of adversity to draw us close to truth and the principles upon which it operates. This may occur at first because when our child is emotionally drowning we go to the Lord in desperation "seeking and listening" for answers. The Lord will hear our pleas and send knowledge, perspective, and important truths about a family member—"things as they really are" (Jacob 4:13).

Through the Holy Ghost, profound comfort and truth are available by which to accurately appraise the importance and validity of information we receive on our prodigal's situation. The Holy Ghost can help us sift through the constant flow of information, feedback, accounts, and stories from friends, other family members, agencies, relatives, and neighbors. A throng of questions flows through the mind as these communications arrive. Are my neighbors right? Is my child telling me the truth?

How do I handle this situation? With the marvelous gifts and blessings we have from our Father, we do not need to be in a constant state of flux, changing direction with every new wind blowing information at us.

The gift of the Holy Ghost is just that—a gift. Through this gift we are taught and instructed in truth: "And by the power of the Holy Ghost ye may know the truth of all things" (Moroni 10:5). Through the power of the Holy Ghost we may be comforted: we may find "righteousness, and peace, and joy in the Holy Ghost" (Romans 14:17). Through the Holy Ghost testimonies are strengthened.

We can trust in the counsel received through the Holy Ghost. A certain father knew that the Lord's words were true and did not concern himself with others' fears. For over five years he patiently listened to the advice of others until he finally said: "I know what the Lord has guaranteed me if I follow his course. What are your guarantees?"

Righteousness

Obedience to the Lord is the beginning of all righteousness. Obedience is possible because God has ordained laws for our progress and we have been endowed with agency. Our love for our Father in Heaven is displayed by our obedience. He asks us to keep his commandments that he may bless us. When we yield our agency to him, we put away the natural man. "We are called upon to purify our inner feelings, to change our hearts, to make our outward actions and appearance conform to what we say we believe and feel inside" (Howard W. Hunter, *Ensign*, May 1992, p. 61).

My (Janice's) nine-year-old daughter walked around the neighborhood and gathered all the pretty rocks she could find. She washed and cleaned them so they would look their best. She then sorted the rocks and mounted her favorite ones on a large orange sheet of construction paper. She was so proud of the different kinds, shapes, and sizes of rocks in her collection. Like my daughter we all have our own "rock collections." We collect our rocks as we journey through life. We polish them, clean them, sort and size them, and label them. We have our "straightforward" rocks, our "determined" rocks, our "caring" rocks, our "see-it-like-it-is" rocks, and our "get-the-job-done" rocks. We are proud of our collection.

Sometimes, however, when someone threatens us we pick up a rock and throw it at him. We justify our action with the label on the rock. The problem is that we may also inadvertently throw these rocks at our children who are already battered and bleeding, or at anyone who disagrees with us, even if the person is trying to help. Our pride will not let us see our rocks as they really are: "tactlessness," "stubbornness," "manipulation," "criticism," or "self-righteousness."

One by one we need to take our rocks and throw them away. For the sake of our children as well as of ourselves we must discard the natural man and choose the Lord's way. Elder Neal A. Maxwell has expressed it thus: "Letting go of the world requires not only deliberate disengagement from the ways of the world, but also being willing to take the next step by yielding to the enticings of the Spirit" (*Nothwithstanding My Weakness* [Salt Lake City: Deseret Book Co., 1981], p. 74). The trailhead to righteousness is surrender, as Elder Robert L. Backman pointed out:

> What Christ desires from each of us is surrender, complete and total—a voluntary gift of trust, faith, and love. C. S. Lewis captured the spirit of this surrender:
> "Christ says, 'Give me All. I don't want so much of your time and so much of your money and so much of your work: I want You. I have not come to torment your natural self, but to kill it. No half-measures are any good. I don't want to cut off a branch here and a branch there, I want to have the whole tree down. . . . Hand over the whole natural self, all the desires which you think

innocent as well as the ones you think wicked—the whole outfit.
I will give you a new self instead. In fact, I will give you Myself:
my own will shall become yours.'" (*Mere Christianity* [New York:
Collier Books, 1960], p. 167.) (*Ensign*, November 1991, p. 10.)

Gospel of Peace

Light and peace are the opposites of darkness and fear. Paul
states that Christ "is our peace" (Ephesians 2:14). And in the
Doctrine and Covenants the Savior says: "Behold, I am Jesus
Christ, the Son of God. I am the same that came unto mine
own, and mine own received me not. I am the light which
shineth in darkness, and the darkness comprehendeth it not."
(D&C 6:21.)

Light will always overcome darkness. This principle is
quickly demonstrated every time you enter a dark room and
turn on the light. Christ is our way, our truth, and our light: "I
am the light of the world: He that followeth me shall not walk
in darkness, but shall have the light of life" (John 8:12).

As we behave in a Christlike manner in our homes, we are
ambassadors of peace and beacons of light. Becoming a light is a
process of adding oil to our lamp so that it can dispel the darkness. We add oil to our lamp drop by drop: an act of service, a
word of kindness or encouragement, the words "I love you," and
the actions to prove it. As we put our drops of oil in the lamp,
our Savior through his grace adds his drops of oil. And so, grace
by grace, we grow in discipleship—line upon line, precept upon
precept.

As parents of a prodigal, we need this precious oil in our
lamps more now than at any other time in our lives. We can reflect the Light of the World, Jesus Christ, to draw our children
back to his fold and our family (see D&C 11:28).

In Victor Hugo's famous novel *Les Miserables*, it's easy to see
the "oil" that the bishop, Monseigneur Bienvenu, puts into his
lamp. *Les Miserables* is the story of Jean Valjean, who was sent to

prison for stealing a loaf of bread to feed his sister and her hungry children. When he entered prison he was gentle, simple, and kind. After nineteen years in prison he has become hard, bitter, and full of hate. When he enters the bishop's home following his release from prison, he is shown kindness and love, and this brings on a struggle within him. But the results of the years of imprisonment win out, and he steals the household's silver plates and silver ladle and runs off with them.

The next day he is back again—law-enforcement officers have caught him and he must now face the bishop. Jean has told the officers that the silver was a gift. Quickly seeing how the land lies, the bishop welcomes Jean Valjean back and asks him why he did not take the candlesticks too, which he says were also a gift.

When the officers are satisfied and leave, the bishop takes down from the mantelpiece the two silver candlesticks and gives them to Jean as he says: "Jean Valjean, my brother, you belong no longer to evil, but to good. It is your soul that I am buying for you. I withdraw it from dark thoughts and from the spirit of perdition, and I give it to God." (Victor Hugo, *Les Miserables*, translated by Charles E. Wilbour [New York: Amsco School Publications, Inc., n.d.], p. 84.)

How symbolic the candlesticks are that are used to buy Jean's soul from darkness! Candlesticks are holders of light. We also have gifts of silver to help purchase our children out of darkness, gifts that belong to our household—love, happiness, joy, and peace. These gifts must be held in the candlestick the Lord has provided, the gospel of Jesus Christ. What joy we will feel when we can say to our child, "Your spirit belongs no more to the dark!"

One sure light meter by which to confirm that light is emanating from us is the presence of the Spirit. The Holy Ghost brings forth certain fruits. "The fruit of the Spirit is love, joy, peace, longsuffering, gentleness, goodness, faith, meekness, temperance" (Galatians 5:22–23). If we possess these traits, we belong to Christ and give light and peace.

Two particular fruits of the Spirit are love and peace. In our homes and in our lives we can create a safe harbor with a lighthouse that emits the light and peace of Christ to safely guide our children home.

When defiant children leave us and associate with certain friends they step into a world filled with evil and veiled distractions. Satan has a cunning way of whetting their appetites and disguising sin. They are surrounded by darkness and their senses become dulled so that they temporarily do not feel the fear, anxiety, turmoil, and pain. All they feel are the thrills, excitements, instant gratifications, and freedoms. They do not notice that they are out in the storm and that the waves are high and crashing against them; they laugh as they are tossed to and fro, thinking it is a game. They do not see the leaks in their boat.

We see the leaks; we see the danger; and we become fearful. We rush out to rescue them from the storm. Often, however, we are so anxious to rescue them that we leave the safety of our own spiritual harbor, and out in the storm we become vulnerable and susceptible. As we are tossed about by powerful emotional waves of anger, guilt, and fear, our emotions tend to rule us instead of our ruling them. We can feel ourselves sinking and we begin to play by the rules of the world: control, money, power, intimidation, contention, fear, addiction, and codependency.

The commandments of the Lord are the sea walls that protect our spiritual harbor and help to keep the storms of the world out. The commandments teach us to be patient, kind, gentle, long-suffering, and tolerant. The commandments also help to light the beacon of Christ. When his beacon shines in our home, our children can see it from every direction and be guided back to safety. Maybe not tomorrow, or next month, or even next year, but eventually the light will bring them back. These are children of light. They have been reserved and spared to come forth in this day. They have a mission to perform. For a time they have forgotten and are now lost, but their eternal spirits have not forgotten.

Faith

One of the greatest tests we can face in this life is whether we will be obedient to the Lord's commandments in all circumstances. At such a difficult time as the months and years of a son's or daughter's waywardness our faith can be tried to the very limits of our endurance.

The Book of Mormon contains an excellent example of the linkage between faith and obedience. When Lehi sent his sons back to Jerusalem to get the plates, the two oldest responded quite differently from the two youngest. Laman and Lemuel murmured, and returned only out of duty. Nephi (and apparently Sam) believed his father and trusted in the Lord. Despite the arduous assignment Nephi said, "I will go and do," and he went and did. Nephi went on to clarify why he was willing to go: "because I know. . . ." (1 Nephi 3:7.) Nephi responded with intelligent faith, not "blind" faith. His knowledge marked the bitter path and sustained his faith in this difficult task. The ability to do, to execute, to complete, to persist, is materially enhanced by intelligent faith.

The crucial role that faith plays in our ability to respond to life's ups and downs is somewhat analogous to flying an airplane. A pleasant, smooth flight often changes abruptly because of turbulence—sometimes becoming a terrifying free-fall caused by a downdraft. Flying at a "faith altitude" of eighteen thousand feet at that moment of turbulence allows considerable room to fall, gain control, and climb again. Flying at eight thousand feet, however, leaves little room for correction and recovery before the next episode. It is often the case when dealing with a wayward child that the episodes of conflict and strife come at unpredictable intervals, sometimes for long periods of time. It seems that just when things begin to smooth out, a downdraft hits. A concerted effort to build faith and testimony during the respites therefore is essential strategy for survival.

Mighty faith and testimony are the hallmark of our prophet

heroes, but even the strongest have been known to question, and possibly attempt to counsel the Lord. Job, a great man of patience and endurance, was chastened for uttering "words without knowledge" (Job 38:2). He struggled as few have done, but still he was able to maintain this strong testimony: "For I know that my redeemer liveth, and that he shall stand at the latter day upon the earth: and though after my skin worms destroy this body, yet in my flesh shall I see God" (Job 19:25–26).

Job knew through a burning witness of the Spirit that God lives. It is the underpinning of faith and testimony to know and understand that we are the offspring of eternal parents, that God is our Father. It is equally important to know his attributes and to understand that he is the embodiment of knowledge, faith, justice, judgment, mercy, and truth. The Prophet Joseph Smith explained:

> It is . . . important that men should have the idea of the existence of the attribute mercy in the Deity, in order to exercise faith in him for life and salvation; for without the idea of the existence of this attribute in the Deity, the spirits of the saints would faint in the midst of the tribulations, afflictions, and persecutions which they have to endure for righteousness' sake. But when the idea of the existence of this attribute is once established in the mind it gives life and energy to the spirits of the saints, believing . . . that the mercy of God will lay hold of them and secure them in the arms of his love, so that they will receive a full reward for all their sufferings. (*Lectures on Faith* 4:15.)

A great aspect of the Atonement is that Christ endured the agonizing punishment justice demanded for all of our sins. Thus he can say, "The Son of Man hath descended below them all" (D&C 122:8). At any time during the whole ordeal he could have put an end to it. During Gethsemane when he was enduring an agony we cannot even begin to comprehend, and when his enemies took him, and beat him, and spat upon him, and when the soldiers placed a crown of thorns on his head, he could have concluded that cruel mockery at any time. As he hung on the cross, exposed and vulnerable, many in the throng mocked and jeered him. He could have stopped it. As he was enduring acute physical pain from the nails in his hands and feet the emotional and spiritual suffering of Gethsemane came back to him. Finally, in order for the sacrifice to be complete, the Father withdrew his comforting presence. At any point, from the time when he entered the garden to that of his death, Christ could have used his immense power to terminate this ordeal. He did not. He suffered it all. The statement he made was precise and explicit. "It is finished" (John 19:30). He did not end it or leave it until it was finished.

In our own much less intense sufferings we too face our own Gethsemane and cry out "Abba, Father, all things are possible unto thee; take away this cup from me" (Mark 14:36). We face our own crucible and cry out again, "My God, my God, why hast thou forsaken me?" (Matthew 27:46.) This suffering can be the great trial of one's life. The test is passed if we are willing to say as the Savior said, "Nevertheless not what I will, but what thou wilt" (Mark 14:36). We too, at any time, can withdraw physically, emotionally or spiritually. But we need to fulfill our mission and endure until we can also say, "It is finished." Our knowledge, faith, and testimony in the gospel preserve us and act as a mainstay in our powers to endure. "A testimony grows," said Elder Milton R. Hunter, "through a person's humility, willingness to submit to God's will, and continuous obedience. The more completely one conforms his life to the teachings of the Master, the greater will be his testimony and the manifestations of the gift of the Spirit." (In Elizabeth Schoenfeld, *Thoughts for an LDS Mother* [Salt Lake City: Bookcraft, 1967], pp. 78–79.)

Our testimonies are never dormant. "A testimony is not a work that is merely completed and concluded. Indeed, it is a process in continuous development. Nourishing and strengthening our testimonies is essential to our spiritual survival." (Helvecio Martins, *Ensign*, November 1990, p. 26.) As we accumulate and employ knowledge, we strengthen faith and testimony and ascend to higher levels of capabilities and spiritual gifts. Elder Richard G. Scott further explained:

> We see such a limited part of the eternal plan He has fashioned for each one of us. Trust Him, even when in eternal perspective it temporarily hurts very much. Have patience when you are asked to wait when you want immediate action. He may ask you to do things which are powerfully against your will. Exercise faith and say, Let Thy will be done. Such experiences, honorably met, prepare you and condition you for yet greater blessings. As your Father, His purpose is your eternal happiness, your continuing development, your increasing capacity. His desire is to share with you all that He has. The path you are to walk through life may be very different from others. You may not always know why He does what He does, but you can know that He is perfectly just and perfectly merciful. He would have you suffer no consequence, no challenge, endure no burden that is superfluous to your good.
>
> To gain unshakable faith in Jesus Christ is to flood your life with brilliant light. You are no longer alone to struggle with challenges you know you cannot resolve or control yourself, for He said, "If ye will have faith in me ye shall have power to do whatsoever thing is expedient in me" (Moroni 7:33). (*Ensign*, November 1991, p. 86.)

Salvation

The straight and narrow pathway to salvation is paved with our service. President Ezra Taft Benson observed, "Christlike service exalts" (*Come, Listen to a Prophet's Voice* [Salt Lake City: Deseret Book Co., 1990], p. 75).

The saving power of service was effectively illustrated during a Relief Society lesson, when one sister had this to say: "I was going through one of the darkest times of my life. It's a wonder that I was able to notice Sister Smith, who seemed to be having her own set of troubles. I at least had a husband to support me in my grief. She had no one. I felt compassion for her and wrote her a little note expressing concern for her well-being; and told her that I understood the problem she was facing, and sympathized with her.

"Sister Smith received it the next day and tearfully called to thank me. She had reached the end of her rope, and my little note had been just what she needed to hang on. But, in truth, I was the one who was lifted. Knowing I had helped someone else through her pain somehow gave meaning to my life at a time when there was no meaning."

This sister's experience bears out Elder Spencer W. Kimball's comment: "Only when you lift a burden, God will lift your burden. Divine paradox this! The man who staggers and falls because his burden is too great can lighten that burden by taking on the weight of another's burden. You get by giving, but your part of giving must be given first." (*The Teachings of Spencer W. Kimball*, p. 251.)

A divinely offered opportunity for the kind of reciprocal burden-sharing just referred to is temple service. If we are in the proximity of a temple, there is no better place to visit while we are enveloped in a family crisis. There we will receive so much more than we give. "A temple provides a sanctuary away 'from the madding crowd' and from the pressing cares of the world. Perhaps more than any other place, the temple reminds us that although as mortals we are in the world, we are not to be of the world. It helps us to function in the world without being overcome by the world. The more we come to the temple, the less likely we are to be overcome by the world. It is we, not the world, who are to do the overcoming (see D&C 76:53)." (Neal A. Maxwell, *Not My Will, But Thine* [Salt Lake City: Bookcraft, 1988], p. 134.)

In the temple we perform Christlike service by opening the gates of salvation to others who without our work would not have that opportunity. The temple is the Lord's house of service and salvation where we receive his healing balm.

Section 109 of the Doctrine and Covenants gives us broad insight into the promises the temple holds for those who serve there. This section is the dedicatory prayer given at the Kirtland Temple in 1836, but this revealed prayer contains much that can be applied to our temple service today.

We go to the temple to feel the power of the Lord: "That thy glory may rest down upon thy people, and upon this thy house . . . that it may be sanctified and consecrated to be holy, and that thy holy presence may be continually in this house; and that all people who shall enter upon the threshold of the Lord's house may feel thy power, and feel constrained to acknowledge that thou hast sanctified it, and that it is thy house, a place of thy holiness" (vv. 12–13).

We go to the temple to grow: "And that they may grow up in thee, and receive a fulness of the Holy Ghost, and be organized according to thy laws, and be prepared" (v. 15).

We go to the temple for protection: "That no combination of wickedness shall have power to rise up and prevail over thy people upon whom thy name shall be put in this house" (v. 26).

We go to the temple to receive strength: "That thy people may not faint in the day of trouble" (v. 38). And we go to the temple for deliverance: "O Lord, deliver thy people from the calamity of the wicked" (v. 46). "That they may be delivered from the hands of all their enemies" (v. 28).

The temple is an eternal link by which we unite our earthly family, particularly when Satan tries to tear it apart.

Praying Always

Prayer is a beautiful, simple act of communicating with our Father in Heaven. As we yield our hearts to him in prayer, we will be guided in our thoughts. The Lord has asked us to draw close to him through this powerful process. In the 1991 October Conference, Elder Francis M. Gibbons gave a talk on secret prayer. He quoted the Doctrine and Covenants: "Yea, I tell thee, that thou mayest know that there is none else save God that knowest thy thoughts and the intents of thy heart" (D&C 6:16). Then he stated:

It is clear, then, that Satan and his followers, who have been cast out of God's presence and are dead to His spirit, are excluded from those who, by the spirit of prophecy and revelation, may know the thoughts and the intents of our hearts. So, in his wisdom and mercy, God has provided a channel of communication between him and his children on earth that Satan, our common enemy, cannot invade. This is the channel of secret prayer. The significance of this to the Latter-day Saint is profound, for by this means we are able to communicate with our Heavenly Father in secrecy, confident that the adversary cannot intrude. . . .

But while Satan can convey thoughts, he does not know whether these thoughts have taken root unless they are reflected either in words or in actions.

All this suggests that we should be wise in what we say and do. We should also be wise in the way we guard precious things that are revealed to us through the Spirit. . . .

Often, we talk too much. We say things that need not be said or should not be said; for in saying them, we may open a crevice which enables Lucifer to wedge his way into our lives. . . . Satan and his followers are persistent in their quest to drag us down to their level. They will use any device or artifice to accomplish their end. (*Ensign*, November 1991, pp. 78–79.)

What a divine tool the Lord has given parents to help them through these difficult times! It's hard to imagine how parents would be able to cope with wayward children without secret prayer. Through it we may fully express our feelings, our fears, concerns, guilt, sorrow, anger, and frustration concerning a rebellious child. What a sweet gift it is, especially at difficult times, to be able to be in constant communication with our Heavenly Father.

Elder Bruce R. McConkie explained:

Prayer—a blessed, blessed prayer—is a gift of God offered by a loving and gracious Father to all his children. It is the means provided for earth's pilgrims, far from their heavenly home and shut out from the personal presence of Him who sent them on their journey, to report their labors and receive further direction. The

Father of us all spoke to each of us personally in the realms of glory whence we came. Now, in this sphere of toil and trial and testing, he offers to continue his speech if we will abide the law that makes such possible. That law is prayer. . . . All three members of the Godhead are involved in and concerned with our prayers. . . . We worship and pray to the Father, in the name of the Son, by the power of the Holy Ghost. (*A New Witness for the Articles of Faith* [Salt Lake City: Deseret Book Co., 1985], pp. 378, 380.)

The Lord has given us the gift of divine association through prayer. We know that all righteous prayers are heard and answered. But again, they are answered according to the Lord's timetable. He chooses how, where, and when he will answer. So often during difficult times the Lord will take the opportunity to tutor us and propel us spiritually forward. We are given an open door to see if we will "do all things whatsoever the Lord . . . shall command [us]" (Abraham 3:25). Elder Richard G. Scott tells of such an experience:

There were then, as now, constantly new lessons. Well do I remember the first time when, as I pled with the Lord for the help and guidance and feeling of support I had come to cherish, there was no answer. Instead I felt a barrier—an insurmountable wall. I reviewed my life, my feelings, my acts—anything that could affect such communication—and found no problems. It was not until after more purposeful struggling that there came the clarification. What I had felt was not a wall but a giant step—an opportunity to rise to a higher spiritual plane, an opportunity evidencing trust that I would obey correct principles without the necessity of constant reinforcement. After more effort, the peaceful comforting presence of the Spirit returned. (In *Hope* [Salt Lake City: Deseret Book Co., 1988], p. 165.)

Lamentation for a Prodigal

In the depths of sorrow
I cry for my prodigal:

"Are there any answers?"
"Is there any hope?"
"Is there anyone that can help?"
This thought emerges:
Pray as He prayed.
Our Father which art in heaven.

Yes, He is there.
But, what words to use
For me to honor Him?
Hallowed be thy name.

Is it really possible—
Families together forever?
Is now too soon?
Thy kingdom come.

How can I
Get through this day?
How can I
Help my child today?
Thy will be done in earth,
As it is in heaven.

Where do I obtain strength
And endure the unendurable?
Give us this day our
Daily bread.

How can I ever
Shed my contempt
For contributors to my sorrow?
Must I?
And forgive us our debts,
As we forgive our debtors.

Can I hold my tongue
That thy will be done?
And lead us not into temptation.

When forces of evil
Encompass me about,
How can I get out?
But deliver us from evil.

Because He loves my prodigal
Far greater than do I,
Because he has the power
Far greater than do I,
I give Him all my thanks,
Adoration, praise,
And worship.
For thine is the kingdom,
And the power,
And the glory, forever.
Amen.
                                        —Mathew Chalker

With All Perseverance

It is true that we must be prepared to ride out the storm and persevere. When we hear the word *persevere* we often picture the pioneers crossing the plains, stalwart and firm in the faith, with a singleness of purpose. They were all of these things. There is another picture, however, this one of the father and his children standing over the fresh grave of the mother and mourning her loss. They plodded forward, but they took the time to grieve.

The Savior has been called the Man of Sorrows. Part of his suffering as Man of Sorrows came from seeing God's children turn away from all that he was trying to do for them (see Matthew 23:37). Some of the most beautiful passages of scripture are those in which Christ allows us to see his tenderness as he mourns. His sorrow over his unrepentant children illustrates to us the sensitive, deep feelings that accompany divine caring. Our Father makes it plain in many scriptures that he mourns for his wicked sons and daughters. "The God of heaven looked upon the residue of the people [those not living righteously] and he wept. . . . And Enoch said unto the Lord: How is it that thou canst weep, seeing thou art holy, and from all eternity to all eternity? . . . The Lord said unto Enoch: Behold these thy brethren; they are the workmanship of mine own hands . . . I created them. . . . Wherefore should not the heavens weep, seeing they shall suffer?" (Moses 7:28–29, 32, 37.)

Also with us, his children, circumstances occur in our lives when we must grieve. A distraught father said of his prodigal: "I couldn't understand what was taking place within me. I would be driving to work and the tears would come from nowhere. I would see a young girl that looked like her, a memory would flash into mind, and I would be unable to continue. It took me a while to realize I was going through many of the same feelings I would have had if she had physically died."

The Lord has given us tears as an escape valve so that we will not break under the strain. Tears are gentle purifiers that cleanse our system of grief and pain. We need not be ashamed to mourn the real though spiritual loss of a loved one.

Jesus Christ trod all over the dusty roads of Judaea and Samaria to find as many disciples as would follow him, showing us yet another side of his divine caring. Yes, he sorrowed for the lost sheep, but he also nurtured and rejoiced over those that followed. The scriptures also teach there is "a time to weep and a time to laugh" (Ecclesiastes 3:4). If we are to persevere, both emotions, sorrow and rejoicing, need to be expressed; each feeling has its place in the blueprint of our nature. Again, there has to be an ongoing emotional release of our excess feelings. Anger is destructive and leaves us hating ourselves, and being constantly downcast makes us hard to live with. If we can laugh or even smile, we can release pent-up emotion in a harmless and helpful way. Victor E. Frankl speaks of his concentration camp experience, commenting on how vital it was to be able to see the humorous side and laugh at the absurd.

> Humor was another of the soul's weapons in the fight for self-preservation. It is well known that humor, more than anything else in the human make-up, can afford an aloofness and an ability to rise above any situation, even if only for a few seconds. I practically trained a friend of mine who worked next to me on the building site to develop a sense of humor. I suggested to him that we would promise each other to invent at least one amusing story daily. . . . The attempt to develop a sense of humor and to see things in a humorous light is some kind of a trick learned while mastering the art of living. (*Man's Search for Meaning* [New York: Pocket Books, 1984], pp. 63–64.)

Scripture advises, "be of good cheer" (D&C 61:36). Being of good cheer, however, does not mean that you have to be constantly laughing and joking when your heart is broken. It can mean something as simple as getting out of bed every morning and getting on with the day. It can mean prohibiting depression from entering into your heart and mind. It can mean facing each day courageously. It can mean looking for the good in life. We need to savor the sweet moments life offers: a walk in the park with our daughter; a kiss from our toddler; or a son performing his priesthood duty well. Look for those little pockets of light when it seems as if darkness is all around.

Elder Marvin J. Ashton has suggested:

> The companionship of good cheer is possible through keeping the commandments of God, not through rationalization. We must commit ourselves to principles and not live by comparison or excuses. Horace Mann wisely said, "In vain do they talk of happiness who never subdued an impulse in obedience to a principle" (From *Common School Journal,* quoted in *Horace Mann:*

His Ideas and Ideals, comp. Joy Elmer Morgan [Washington, D.C.: National Home Library Foundation, 1936], p. 149). . . .

Being of good cheer makes it possible for us to turn all of our sunsets into sunrises. With good cheer, carrying our cross can be our ladder to happiness. When Jesus comes into our lives, cheer lights the way. How powerful and comforting is the Savior's declaration, "In the world ye shall have tribulation: but be of good cheer; I have overcome the world" (John 16:33). (*Be of Good Cheer* [Salt Lake City: Deseret Book Co., 1987], pp. 6–7.)

Scriptural Swords and Other Lessons

The scriptures can supply additional plates of armor during a prodigal crisis. It is interesting that Paul refers to the scriptures as a sword: "And the sword of the Spirit, which is the word of God" (Ephesians 6:17). (You can almost hear clanging swords as we battle against the evils of the latter days.) To keep ourselves strong and prepared to face this battle we must daily drink from this well of spiritual strength. President Spencer W. Kimball expressed this need thus: "I find that when I get casual in my relationships with divinity and when it seems that no divine ear is listening and no divine voice is speaking, that I am far, far away. If I immerse myself in the scriptures the distance narrows and the spirituality returns." (*The Teachings of Spencer W. Kimball,* p. 135.)

There is no problem that cannot be solved when we combine sincere prayer with careful studying and pondering of the scriptures. "There is no question—personal or social or political or occupational—that need go unanswered. Therein [in the scriptures] is contained the fulness of the everlasting gospel. Therein we find principles of truth that will resolve every confusion and every problem and every dilemma that will face the human family or any individual in it." (Boyd K. Packer, *Teach the Scriptures* [Salt Lake City: Church Educational System, 1978], p. 5.) The scriptures cut through all the philosophies and traditions of child rearing, bringing us to the essentials of truth.

The scriptures contain guidance for dealing with the stresses brought on by wayward children. One of the great stress-producing perplexities concerning ungovernable children is the issue of discipline. Nothing seems to split parents apart like philosophies of discipline. Each partner comes consciously or unconsciously to the marriage with a style of discipline, and rarely are the styles compatible. Yet there must be unity if parents are to survive and succeed.

"Reproving betimes with sharpness" (D&C 121:43) is an instructive yet often misunderstood scripture on discipline. The scriptural examples of the Savior reproving someone show that his intentions were only to enlighten and lift the person being reproved; he never vented feelings of frustration. *Reprove* means to correct with kindly intent, *betimes* means quickly or immediately, and *sharpness* means with clarity or distinctness, not causticly or harshly. Properly applied, these scriptures give us critically needed advice on how to instruct and correct our children.

Defiant and disobedient children will often act hostile, resentful, and bitter toward us. In their anger they can be abusive, profane, vulgar, and aggressive, thereby turning our safe harbor into a contentious sea of chaos. The Book of Mormon has given us important insights in handling this delicate problem. Alma points out that we have the right to protect our home—"the Nephites were taught to defend themselves . . . yea, and they were also taught never to give an offense" (Alma 48:14). Behavior that is seen as offensive will usually provoke a powerful reaction that is contrary to the purposes of our home and stewardship. Paul, an apostle of the ancient Church, also taught us never to give offense: "Fathers, provoke not your children" (Ephesians 6:4). While we should not tolerate abuse toward us or other family members, the applicable guiding principles in the scriptures are self-control and patience. "The scriptures have the power to speak to our particular situations wherever we are in life. The insights you gain may be entirely different from the ones that I gain, but they all can strengthen us personally." (Ruth B. Wright, *Ensign*, November 1990, p. 78.)

Reading the scriptures brings promised blessings to the whole family. If you are struggling with your testimony, read the Book of Mormon. If you are having marital problems, read the Book of Mormon. If your children are not speaking to you, read the Book of Mormon. If there is constant fighting in your home, read the Book of Mormon. If there is vulgarity and profanity in your home, read the Book of Mormon. If you desire to have a loving home and if you desire to have the pure love of Christ in your home, read the Book of Mormon. This is the counsel Elder Marion G. Romney gave:

> I feel certain that if, in our homes, parents will read from the Book of Mormon prayerfully and regularly, both by themselves and with their children, the spirit of that great book will come to permeate our homes and all who dwell therein. The spirit of reverence will increase; mutual respect and consideration for each other will grow. The spirit of contention will depart. Parents will counsel their children in greater love and wisdom. Children will be more responsive and submissive to that counsel. Righteousness will increase. Faith, hope, and charity—the pure love of Christ—will abound in our homes and lives, bringing in their wake peace, joy, and happiness. (Quoted by President Ezra Taft Benson in *Ensign*, May 1986, p. 6.)

Another recurring lesson gleaned from parents with troublesome children is best explained with the following analogy. Earthquakes are measured by a sensitive instrument called a seismograph. Small earthquakes (tremors) are rather frequent and don't cause much damage. Major earthquakes, however, can cause tremendous damage. Sometimes it may seem that our house sits right on top of an active fault and that our children put us through earthquakes of varying sizes. It is vital for parents to be able to distinguish between tremors and major quakes.

Each parent's seismograph is calibrated differently, becoming more accurate as experiences accumulate. The trick is to respond in a manner commensurate with the size of the earthquake. If we drain our stamina in dealing with the tremors, we will not have the emotional or spiritual energy necessary to handle the big quakes. Ask yourself, "Is this problem of an eternal nature that can damage their lives?" If the answer is no, then recognize that you are in earthquake country and try to save your emotions for a major quake.

In this context Elder Marvin J. Ashton has given some wise counsel on communication in our families:

> Communication in the family will often be a sacrifice because we are expected to use our time, our means, our talents, and our patience to impart, share, and understand. Too often we use communication periods as occasions to tell, dictate, plead, or threaten. Nowhere in the broadest sense should communication in the family be used to impose, command, or embarrass.
>
> To be effective, family communication must be an exchange of feelings and information. . . . Time and participation on the part of all are necessary ingredients. In family discussions, differences should not be ignored, but should be weighed and evaluated calmly. One's point or opinion usually is not as important as a healthy, continuing relationship. Courtesy and respect in listening and responding during discussions are basic. . . . How important it is to know how to disagree with another's point of view without being disagreeable. . . .
>
> Try to be understanding and not critical. Don't display shock, alarm, or disgust with others' comments or observations. Don't react violently. Work within the framework of a person's free agency. Convey the bright and optimistic approach.
>
> I pray our Heavenly Father will help us to communicate more effectively in the home through a willingness to sacrifice, a willingness to listen, a willingness to vocalize feelings, . . . a willingness to practice patience. "How forcible are right words!" (Job 6:25.) Yes, how forcible are right words shared at the right moment with the right person. (*Ensign*, May 1976, pp. 52, 54.)

Armor of Unity

Parental unity is essential to making home a safe and inviting harbor. Righteous unity allows us to pull down the very powers of heaven when a prodigal crisis threatens to produce disunity. Eventually a recalcitrant child will be able to see and feel the stark contrast between the world and the peace of a gospel-centered home. Unity in some homes may currently be out of reach. If such is your circumstance, be at peace: "God . . . knowest . . . the intents of [the] heart" (D&C 6:16). We all know of families in which marital difficulties exist but for the sake of a child the parents are able to set aside their problems, pull together, and save that child—and save themselves also. The Lord recognizes the sacrifice and rewards it accordingly.

Family unity is easier achieved by parents who look for the good in each other. Elder N. Eldon Tanner wrote: "Let us look for the good rather than try to discover any hidden evil. We can easily find fault in others if that is what we are looking for. Even in families, divorce has resulted and families have been broken up because the husband or wife was looking for and emphasizing the faults rather than loving and extolling the virtues of the other." (*Ensign*, July 1972, p. 35.)

> *I was so troubled when I began to see a particular negative trait occurring in my children that had been passed on to them by my spouse. The distress worsened as my children married and I could see this trait creating problems in their marriages. I began to be angry at myself for having married this person and giving my children this parent. The Lord comforted me by placing within my mind this realization: I was to look at the wonderful traits and gifts my husband passed on to my children. When I did this, I realized that my children had gained many outstanding qualities from him that only he could give them. I was greatly comforted by the recognition that somehow the Lord is willing to work within the framework of all our weaknesses.*

To stand united in marriage does not mean that one spouse must become a clone of the other. Each of us brings special gifts to the partnership. For example, in a marriage known to the authors, the husband has always been a "morning person" while the wife is a "night person." Frequently on Saturdays, to give his wife a treat, he takes the children to breakfast and runs errands so she can sleep in. Conversely, she waits up for the dating teenagers and lets her husband sleep. The heavy load that parents have will pull much easier if they are yoked together.

The Lord wants us to be one in marriage as the Godhead is one; "that you may be one, even as I have commanded you" (D&C 51:9).

> With all the divisions, and all the discontent, and the quarrelings and opposition among the powers on earth, or that have been revealed from heaven, I have never heard that it has ever been revealed to the children of men that there was any division between God the Father, God the Son, and God the Holy Ghost. They are one. They always have been one. They always will be one, from eternity unto eternity. . . . In the celestial kingdom of God there is oneness—there is union. (Wilford Woodruff, *Millennial Star*, 52 [1890]: 577.)

This is a principle of truth: as we grow to be one, so also the love and influence we have over our children grows. Our children are pulled and drawn to the pure love and true happiness they feel. On the other hand, if parents are divided they run the risk of being conquered. As one beleaguered father of teenagers said to his irate wife: "Stop treating me like the enemy. I'm the only one in this house on your side." As you lift and pull together it will make the burden lighter. Then each of you can relieve the other for much-needed emotional and spiritual breaks. "Somehow, some way," said Elder James E. Faust, "we must try harder to make our homes stronger so that they will stand as sanctuaries against the unwholesome, pervasive moral dry rot around us. Harmony, happiness, peace, and love in the home can help give children the required inner strength to cope with life's challenges." (*Ensign*, November 1990, p. 33.)

As a couple, parents need to humble themselves and bend

their attitudes to the will of the Lord. When we are able to do this there will be a feeling of peace and harmony in our homes. We need the power to see "things as they are . . . and as they are to come" (D&C 93:24). When we can see spouse and children through our spiritual eyes we can increase the harmony and happiness in our home. Then we are able to draw the rebellious child like a magnet into the circle of influence that will carry through this life and into eternity.

Single parents may feel that they carry a lopsided load in raising their children, particularly wayward ones. The solution is to yoke yourself with Christ. All of the promises, blessings, help, insight, and comfort are available whether you are divorced, widowed, married to an active Latter-day Saint or to a less-active spouse, or married to someone of another faith. For a time, unity may be a partnership between you and the Lord. The Lord will prepare a way for you to cope and succeed with the added responsibility. We have all seen and read about the strength and courage of single parents.

The greatest example that we, the authors, have seen of this brand of fortitude was our own mother. She was married to someone not of her faith—an "anti-Mormon," to be precise. However, she used all of her strength, time, skills, and gifts to influence her children to choose the gospel of Jesus Christ. She was willing to give of her time and energy to make sure we associated with Latter-day Saint friends; she held parties at our home and got involved in our activities. She prayerfully listened to the whisperings of the Spirit.

She was obedient to the Church leaders. For example, when I (Janice) was fifteen and a half, the First Presidency sent out a letter regarding dating. It stated that young people should not date until the age of sixteen. I had already been dating for six months, but Mother said, "The Church says you shouldn't date until you're sixteen, so you won't." At the time it seemed pretty stupid to me. I had already been dating, and it was only six months until my birthday, so why not let it go? But Mother insisted that we obey the prophet, and we did.

Her most important priority was that her children marry the right person in the temple. She told each of us, "It will hurt me not to be able to attend the temple and see you married, but it will hurt me more, if you didn't marry in the temple."

As with all families, we have had our difficulties, but each of Mother's children has married a member of the Church and she has sent out two missionaries. We are all grateful for the greatest gift Mother ever gave us, the opportunity to receive a testimony of the gospel of Jesus Christ.

Although we are engaged in a battle against darkness and evil, the forces of righteousness will prevail. Some of the pieces of armor God has given us to win this battle are recapped below.

1. Be aware of the opposition and the tools that Satan employs.
2. Know and believe that God is all-powerful and will win.
3. Trust that the Holy Ghost can reveal truths about your child.
4. Put off the natural man if you want to survive and recover.
5. Become an ambassador of peace and light to draw your children to you.
6. Strengthen your testimony; it is essential to your spiritual survival.
7. Practice Christlike service; it can heal and exalt.
8. Pray always.
9. Do not be ashamed to mourn.
10. Allow yourself to laugh and be of good cheer.
11. Read the scriptures; this will bring blessings to the whole family.
12. Keep the channels of communication open.
13. Remember that unity is essential to making your home a safe and inviting harbor.

4

Sweet Are the Uses
of Adversity

Joseph Smith experienced the First Vision when he was fourteen years of age and was martyred at age thirty-eight. The intervening twenty-four years were a concentration of significant life experiences—including a considerable amount of tribulation. Brigham Young informs us that it was the suffering, sorrow, and tribulation that brought Joseph to exaltation: "Joseph could not have been perfected, though he had lived a thousand years, if he had received no persecution. If he had lived a thousand years, and led this people, and preached the Gospel without persecution, he would not have been perfected as well as he was at the age of thirty-nine years." (In *Journal of Discourses* 2:7.)

The Doctrine and Covenants discloses a great deal about Joseph's development from spiritual infancy to exemplary maturity. For example, in 1829 the Lord said to Joseph, "Be firm in keeping the commandments wherewith I have commanded you; and if you do this, behold I grant unto you eternal life, even if you should be slain" (D&C 5:22). (Incidentally, this is the same blessing that we have been offered through temple ordinances.) A few years later these glorious promises were given to Joseph:

For I am the Lord thy God, and will be with thee even unto the end of the world, and through eternity; for verily I seal upon you your exaltation, and prepare a throne for you in the kingdom of my Father, with Abraham your father. Behold, I have seen your sacrifices, and will forgive all your sins; I have seen your sacrifices in obedience to that which I have told you. (D&C 132:49–50.)

Joseph had become completely obedient. The Lord could trust him implicitly. In 1842, displaying extraordinary wisdom, Joseph Smith explained: "Whatever God requires is right, no matter what it is, although we may not see the reason thereof till long after the events transpire. If we seek first the kingdom of God, all good things will be added." (*Teachings of the Prophet Joseph Smith* [Salt Lake City: Deseret Book Co., 1938], p. 256.)

When compared to eternity, Joseph's twenty-four years of tribulation truly were short, consistent with the Lord's words, "thine afflictions shall be but a small moment" (D&C 121:7). "Mortal life is temporary and, measured against eternity, infinitesimally brief. If a microscopic droplet of water should represent the length of mortal life, by comparison all the oceans on earth put together would not even begin to represent everlasting life." (Boyd K. Packer, *Ensign*, May 1991, p. 9.) In our premortal experience we understood that this temporal existence would be but a small moment, and weighing this probationary time against eternal rewards, we shouted for joy.

As any parents of a trying child will confirm, our earthly existence will provide us with ample trials and tribulations. Certainly we need not seek them, as President Marion G. Romney said. "This does not mean that we crave suffering. We avoid all we can. However, we now know, and we all knew when we elected to come into mortality, that we would here be proved in the crucible of adversity and affliction." (*Improvement Era*, December 1969, p. 66.) Nor should we rail against adversity when it comes: "Despise not the chastening of the Lord; neither weary of his correction: for whom the Lord loveth he correcteth; even as a father the son in whom he delighteth" (Proverbs 3:11–12). We are here making preparations for eternity. We are always in the process of preparation and can be tested at any time, at any stage of life.

> Adversity in one form or another, is the universal experience of man. It is the common lot of all men to experience misfortune, suffering, sickness, or other adversities. Ofttimes our work is arduous and unnecessarily demanding. Our faith is tried in various ways—sometimes unjustly tried. At times it seems that even God is punishing us and ours. One of the things that makes all this so hard to bear is that we ourselves appear to be chosen for this affliction while others presumably escape these adversities. (A. Theodore Tuttle, *Improvement Era*, December 1967, p. 47.)

Blaine Yorgason's tender poem "The Monument" helps us to grasp the concept that Heavenly Father has placed his trust in each of us. He entrusts us with exacting tasks to overcome before we go back to him. That trust is a confirmation of his love.

The Monument

God,
Before He sent His children to earth,
Gave each of them
A very carefully selected package
Of problems.

These,
He promised, smiling,
Are yours alone. No one
Else may have the blessings
These problems will bring you.

And only you
Have the special talents and abilities
That will be needed

> To make these problems
> Your servants.
>
> Now go down to your birth
> And to your forgetfulness. Know that
> I love you beyond measure.
> These problems I give you
> Are a symbol of that love.
>
> The monument you make of your life
> With the help of your problems
> Will be a symbol of your
> Love for me,
> Your Father.
> (*Charlie's Monument* [Salt Lake City:
> Bookcraft, 1976], p. vi.)

Mortality is tailored to provide each of us with the proper testing and proving. "Every trial and experience you have passed through is necessary for your salvation" (Brigham Young, in *Journal of Discourses* 8:150).

To clarify, there is no desire in this chapter to be like Job's friends and tell you why you are suffering. You alone can receive the answers to this question through inspiration and revelation. We can, though, share what others have learned through their afflictions.

Adversity Brings Experience

When the lives of the Savior, Joseph Smith, and many other archetypes are examined, the ten-letter word *experience* seems utterly inadequate to convey all the ramifications of this primary purpose of earth life.

Contrary to what might be expected, I look back on experiences that at the time seemed especially desolating and painful with particular satisfaction. Indeed, everything I have learned, everything that has truly enhanced and enlightened my existence, has been through affliction and not through happiness. If it ever were to be possible to eliminate affliction from our earthly existence, the result would not be to make life delectable, but to make it too banal and trivial to be endurable. (Malcolm Muggeridge, *A Twentieth Century Testimony*, quoted in *Reader's Digest*, January 1991, p. 158.)

In his book *Man's Search for Meaning* (New York: Pocket Books, 1984), Victor E. Frankl describes an experience in a concentration camp where the men were being punished. They were being forced to go without food the whole day. Because the prisoners were so severely run down, this seemingly minor punishment caused many to become completely desperate.

The Jewish block warden was so concerned that he asked Frankl to give a short inspirational talk to the group. Frankl admits that he wasn't feeling very well himself, but the situation was so critical that he felt he had to make an effort. He tried to talk to them about the future, explaining that things must soon get better. He mentioned their past, and tried to have them focus on good memories. But most of all, he tried to give some meaning to their suffering by quoting from a poet: "What you have experienced, no power on earth can take from you." (See pp. 102–4.)

Having had this experience, Victor E. Frankl, a psychiatrist, later taught, "Suffering ceases to be suffering at the moment it finds a meaning" (p. 135). We also need to find meaning in what we are experiencing, remembering that everyone's "meaning" is going to be different. Personal prayer is one of the best avenues in searching for meaning to your suffering.

Pain stayed so long I said to him today,
"I will not have you with me any more."

I stamped my foot and said, "Be on your way,"
And paused there, startled at the look he wore.
"I, who have been your friend," he said to me,
"I, who have been your teacher—all you know
Of understanding love, of sympathy,
And patience, I have taught you. Shall I go?"
He spoke the truth, this strange unwelcome guest;
I watched him leave, and knew that he was wise.
He left a heart grown tender in my breast,
He left a far, clear vision in my eyes.
I dried my tears, and lifted up a song—
Even for one who'd tortured me so long.
(Quoted in Spencer W. Kimball, *Faith Precedes the Miracle*
[Salt Lake City: Deseret Book Co., 1972], p. 99.)

Jesus Christ learned line upon line, precept upon precept, and grew from grace to grace (see D&C 93:13). Elder Neal A. Maxwell points out that Christ, condescending from his throne on high and being tutored after the manner of the flesh, intellectually understood beforehand the "awesome responsibilities" of the Atonement. But it was his actual performance of atonement (which was required to bring to pass the salvation of man) that meant that he knew experientially the role of Redeemer. (See *Meek and Lowly* [Salt Lake City: Deseret Book Co., 1987], p. 38.) As Augustine said, "God had one son on earth without sin, but never one without suffering" (quoted in *Minute Masterpieces*, Lucy Gertsch, comp. [Salt Lake City: Bookcraft, 1953], p. 106).

When the first child is expected, parents listen intently to all the anecdotes from friends who have already been through it. They know intellectually what it will be like. However, it is not until the actual birth—she to suffer the labor pains, and he to stand by and watch helplessly—that they understand experientially the true price of bearing a child. Elder John Taylor commented on the necessity of passing through the school of experience:

It is necessary, then, that we pass through the school of suffering, trial, affliction, and privation, to know ourselves, to know others, and to know our God. Therefore it was necessary, when the Saviour was upon the earth, that he should be tempted in all points, like unto us, and "be touched with the feeling of our infirmities," to comprehend the weaknesses and strength, the perfections and imperfections of poor fallen human nature. . . .

He knows how to estimate and put a proper value upon human nature, for he having been placed in the same position as we are, knows how to bear with our weaknesses and infirmities, and can fully comprehend the depth, power, and strength of the afflictions and trials that men have to cope with in this world, and thus understandingly and by experience, he can bear with them as a father and an elder brother.

It is necessary, also, inasmuch as we profess that we are aiming at the same glory, exaltation, power, and blessings in the eternal world, that we should pass through the same afflictions, endure the same privations, conquer as he conquered, and overcome as he did, and thus by integrity, truth, virtue, purity, and a high-minded and honorable course before God, angels, and men, secure for ourselves an eternal exaltation in the eternal world, as he did. (In *Journal of Discourses* 1:148–49.)

There really is no substitute for experience. Enduring experience is meant to teach us empathy, knowledge, and insights which can be eternally ours. As the Savior said to the Prophet Joseph Smith and us: "The Son of Man hath descended below them all. Art thou greater than he?" (D&C 122:8.)

These physical losses and tribulations, if endured in His name, have their limits and are refining. The apparently, but not really, limitless mental and spiritual anguish that arises from life's buffetings takes on meaning. Pain becomes a laboratory of soul-nurture, and we may "count it all joy." The darkest abyss has its own revelations, its own chrysalis of higher promise. This is not myth! I testify it is the deepest secret of life. (Truman G. Madsen, *Eternal Man* [Salt Lake City: Deseret Book Co., 1966], p. 60.)

Adversity Teaches Patience

Divine tutoring will always include lessons on patience. Rearing a child who has turned away from you will require long-suffering and patience. You must develop resources of forbearance you didn't even know were possible. "This mortal existence is the Lord's sifting sphere, the time when we are subject to trials, testing, and tribulations. Future rewards will be based on our patient endurance of all things." (Bruce R. McConkie, *Mormon Doctrine*, 2nd ed. [Salt Lake City: Bookcraft, 1966], p. 557.) Paul declared, "We glory in tribulations . . . knowing that tribulation worketh patience" (Romans 5:3).

If we can bear patiently all we are afflicted with, the Lord can work his wonderful miracles on us. "No pang that is suffered by man or woman upon the earth will be without its compensating effect . . . if it be met with patience" (James E. Talmage, as quoted in Spencer W. Kimball, *Faith Precedes the Miracle* [Salt Lake City: Deseret Book Co., 1979], p. 98).

Harry Emerson Fosdick compared pearls and patience:

> The most extraordinary thing about the oyster is this. Irritations get into his shell. He does not like them. But when he cannot get rid of them, he uses the irritation to do the loveliest thing an oyster ever has a chance to do. If there are irritations in our lives today, there is only one prescription: make a pearl. It may have to be a pearl of patience. . . . It takes faith and love to do it." (Quoted by Marvin J. Ashton in *Hope* [Salt Lake City: Deseret Book Co., 1988], p. 21.)

Lean Not unto Thine Own Understanding

At a sacrament meeting, a brother ended his talk by saying: "I thought I knew faith. I had served as bishop; I'd been in the stake presidency; but I never knew faith until I faced that 'black wall.' I had no idea what to do or how to help my son overcome cocaine. I had to put my hand out and say to the Lord, 'Lead me, guide me, walk beside me, help me find the way.'" This brother had learned what so many frantic parents need to realize: when we have tried everything with a child without success, and have reached that black pit of despair, we can put our affairs in God's hands and trust in him.

The Hiding Place is the true story of two Dutch women, sisters, who were subjected to the horrors of a concentration camp. Surprisingly, the book is not about humiliation and sorrow; it is about goodness and triumph. At the end of the book, Corrie ten Boom (the author) has been released from the camp just a few days after her beloved sister had died from the extreme hardships. After first questioning "what if?" she says this: "There are no 'ifs' in God's kingdom . . . his timing is perfect. His will is our hiding place. Lord Jesus, keep me in Your will! Don't let me go mad by poking about outside it." (*The Hiding Place* [New York: Bantam Books, 1974], p. 224.) It was years later when she found out that a "clerical error" had caused her release and that a few days after she had been let go all the women of her age in the camp had been taken to another camp and gassed.

Because she was able to "trust in the Lord with all [her] heart; and lean not unto [her] own understanding" (Proverbs 3:5), she grew spiritually strong and emotionally healthy in her harrowing environment. She was like those President Spencer W. Kimball spoke of: "They who reach down into the depths of life where, in the stillness, the voice of God has been heard, have the stabilizing power which carries them poised and serene through the hurricane of difficulties" (*Ensign*, May 1979, p. 6). Hence the Lord was able to utilize her as a beacon of light. This drew the spiritually starved to the healing blessings the Lord could offer them.

If we are going to survive, if we are going to progress, if we are going to find peace, we must learn to trust the Lord completely.

As difficult and perplexing as it can be, we must summon the faith to place our confidence in him. Of exhibiting this trust, President Ezra Taft Benson has said:

> It is soul-satisfying to know that God is mindful of us and ready to respond when we place our trust in Him and do that which is right. There is no place for fear among men and women who place their trust in the Almighty and who do not hesitate to humble themselves in seeking divine guidance through prayer. Though persecutions arise, though reverses come, in prayer we can find reassurance, for God will speak peace to the soul. That peace, that spirit of serenity, is life's greatest blessing. (*Ensign,* February 1990, p. 5.)

That We May Be Counted Worthy

It is extremely difficult to go through suffering when it is not merited. In *The Hiding Place,* Corrie ten Boom describes how her family became involved in helping the Jews in Holland during World War II to hide and escape the persecution that was occurring. They were instrumental in aiding many Jewish people to escape but they were eventually caught. Their father, who was in his eighties, was offered his release on condition that he promise to stop these activities. He refused to do so, and his daughters never saw him alive again.

These two women, who were in their fifties, were sent to a slave labor camp. They were put in a crowded cattle car with no room to lie down and no privacy. When they got to their destination, they were told to strip off all their clothes to be de-liced and cleaned. The male guards were gawking at and mocking the hundreds of naked bodies. These two cultured Christian spinsters knew they would have to parade before the guards before going to the cold shower. For Corrie, this was the final indignation. She didn't know how she could endure it, until she had a picture come to her mind of the Savior's crucifixion—and suddenly she said to her sister, "Bessie, they took His clothes too." Her degradation turned to triumph; because of Christ's example she was able to bear the humiliation.

Parents dealing with rebellious children must at times endure undeserved debasement and humiliation. Sweet childhood experiences are forgotten by careless children, who may suddenly and openly censure their nurturing parents, calling them hypocrites, child abusers, and liars. Neighbors may gawk at your kids' attire, principals call, and the police show up at your door.

Perhaps it will lessen our humiliation in such circumstances if we remember that the Savior was also misunderstood, falsely accused, and verbally abused by the ones he came to die for. We must learn to bear this without complaint, as he did. It is all a part of enduring to the end in faith. President Brigham Young said:

> If we are ever prepared to enjoy the society of Enoch, Noah, Melchizedek, Abraham, Isaac, and Jacob, or of their faithful children, and of the faithful Prophets and Apostles, we must pass through the same experience, and gain the knowledge, intelligence, and endowments that will prepare us to enter into the celestial kingdom of our Father and God. How many of the Latter-day Saints will endure all these things, and be prepared to enjoy the presence of the Father and the Son? (In *Journal of Discourses* 8:150.)

Elder Howard W. Hunter teaches that the principle of enduring with ever-increasing righteousness is eternal and applies to us today: "Ultimately, what our Father in Heaven will require of us is more than a contribution; it is a total commitment, a complete devotion, all that we are and all that we can be" (*Ensign*, May 1990, p. 60). The Lord has stated: "My people must be tried in all things, that they may be prepared to receive the glory that I have for them, even the glory of Zion" (D&C 136:31).

From the early Christians who died as Nero's entertainment,

to the pioneers who left their warm homes to trudge across icy plains, to our day of the explicit videos, crime, materialism, drugs, and cults, Saints have endured because they believed it was what their Lord required of them. Each age has suffered its own hardships. When Brigham Young spoke to the pioneers who had suffered so much physical hardship, he compared their physical suffering to the great hardship of losing a child spiritually. He told the Saints of his day: Your "troubles and sorrows [brought about by your children] . . . are comparatively trifling, unless your children disregard all your tender solicitude and wise counsels and examples, and, when arrived at maturity, forsake you and go headlong to destruction, when you will think that you never had any trouble until then. The want of bread for them in their infancy was no sorrow, when compared with such a trial." (In *Journal of Discourses* 7:336.)

Elaine Cannon reminds us: "Adversity proves whom God can trust. Who of us, as Job did, will stand firm, be obedient, and love God no matter what comes into our lives?" (*Adversity* [Salt Lake City: Bookcraft, 1987], p. 29.) Adversity helps to enlarge our spiritual integrity. "So that we ourselves glory in you . . . for your patience and faith in all your persecutions and tribulations that ye endure: which is a manifest token of the righteous judgment of God, that ye may be counted worthy of the kingdom of God" (2 Thessalonians 1:4–5).

Adversity Strips Us of Pride

Throughout all dispensations the prophets have denounced pride. It has been referred to as the great sin of the spirit. It can lead to damnation. It would seem, then, that one character trait we should be glad to rid ourselves of is pride. What is it worth to us to remove from our neck this millstone called pride? What would we pay to rid ourselves of this heavy weight that keeps us from rising spiritually to meet our God? What price do we place on gaining the prized attribute of humility? Elder N. Eldon Tanner spoke of those who "want to be popular. . . . and are more concerned with pleasing men than pleasing God." (*Ensign*, November 1975, p. 78.) Elaine L. Jack asked, "Are the comparisons you make of yourself and others based on the model of the Savior's life, or do they come from trying to fit your life into the pattern of others' lives?" (*Ensign*, November 1990, p. 89.) We must resist the pervasive and destructive practice of comparing ourselves with other parents. "We must learn to judge ourselves not by what we are but by what, under the influence of the Lord, we may become" (Richard G. Scott, *Ensign*, November 1979, p. 71).

Adversity of any kind can help us eliminate pride. But the specific tribulation faced by parents who have to watch their youngster destroy himself or herself is particularly well suited to exterminating pride. Pleasing the world ceases to matter when one's child is headed for destruction. Whatever we have to do—beg, borrow, or plead—is not too large a price if it will save the one we love.

Matthew 5:5 says, "Blessed are the meek: for they shall inherit the earth." A footnote in the 1984 LDS revised edition of the Bible suggests that the meek are those who have suffered.

> *A few of us were discussing the trials of raising children. The focus turned to one lady in the group who had just discovered her son was using drugs. She was, of course, completely distraught and didn't have a clue as to what to do next. With my great expertise (my oldest was nine years of age), I spoke up. "Why don't you just make him stop?" She looked at me with such sadness and said, "It just doesn't work that way."*
>
> *A few years later I was having some serious trouble with a teenager. This very same lady called me. (I have always been impressed that not once did she say, "I told you so.") She said, "If you ever need a shoulder to cry on, remember, I've been there." Whenever I see someone sorrowing over a stray child, I try to remember her example.*

Adversity Purifies and Ennobles the Soul

There is a beautiful sloping hill overlooking the Sea of Galilee. Tradition has it that this is the place where the Savior taught his disciples the Beatitudes. In that sermon the Lord connected certain blessings with particular character traits. The one that has the sweetest promise is, "Blessed are the pure in heart, for they shall see God" (Matthew 5:8). Adversity can help us gain that prize, if we grow through it—as well as go through it. Adversity becomes bitter only if we learn nothing from it. Adversity can be a great spiritual purifier. Just as fire can burn out the impurities in metal, so can adversity burn out the impurities in our soul.

> In our own inner experience we can trace the opposite products of pain. At this hour life seems blinding, devastating. Yet it is a measure of our discipleship of Christ that even sorely grievous hours have yielded enlightenment, a budding knowledge of self and others, and ennoblement. When we search ourselves, it is no mystery that good, the purifying force of godliness, may arise out of affliction. (Looking back we may wonder whether anything we really prize comes without it.) (Truman G. Madsen, *Eternal Man*, p. 59.)

Ranell Wallace was a young and pretty woman when she crashed into the side of a mountain in a small, private airplane. She was burned severely, including her face. Anyone familiar with the sufferings of a burn victim can appreciate what the next years were like for this girl in terms of anguish and despair. Not only did she live in constant physical agony, but there was the knowledge of how she appeared to the world. She was forced to wear a face mask to keep her face moist so that it could heal as much as possible. Once when she went into McDonald's to eat, seeing the mask they mistook her for a robber. In front of everyone she was arrested and handcuffed until the police arrived and explanations were made. She has had operation after painful operation to try to help her look more normal. But she has said: "If I could snap my fingers and make it so the whole thing never had happened, I wouldn't do it. Because I remember the person I was before all this happened. All that I have endured has given me so much. Without all I have suffered I would not be the person I am now."

> Researchers at the Yale University School of Medicine "have been impressed by the number of prisoners of the Vietnam war who explicitly claimed that although their captivity was extraordinarily stressful—filled with torture, disease, malnutrition, and solitary confinement—they nevertheless . . . benefitted from the captivity experience, seeing it as a growth experience" (W. H. Sledge, J. A. Boydstun and A. J. Rabe, "Self-Concept Changes Related to War Captivity," quoted in Victor E. Frankl, *Man's Search for Meaning*, p. 171).

There is something elegant about the spirit of one who has been through and learned from suffering. Molinos said, "Thou art never at any time nearer to God than when under tribulation, which he permits for the purification of the soul." As one woman has expressed it: "My sister's husband walked out on her and she raised four boys alone. I watched as she went through so much. Her boys had no dad to guide them, and their mother had to earn the living. The kids got into everything—dope, immorality, you name it. But she pulled them through somehow. Just last year I visited her because one boy was graduating from college. I hold my sister way up on a pedestal." This measure of esteem accords with "man-in-the-street" opinion, as Victor E. Frankl wrote: "Austrian public-opinion pollsters recently reported that those held in highest esteem by most of the people interviewed are neither the great artists nor the great scientists, neither the great statesmen nor the great sports figures, but those who master a hard lot with their heads held high." (*Man's Search for Meaning*, p. 173.)

Adversity Helps Us to Know God

Shortly before our beloved Savior was taken away to be humiliated and tortured, he uttered these oft-quoted words: "And this is life eternal, that they might know thee the only true God, and Jesus Christ, whom thou hast sent" (John 17:3). This statement has a profound and serious message for us. It teaches us the tremendous importance of coming to *know* our Father in Heaven. In the plainest of words our Redeemer asserts that our very future, even our eternal life, depends on how well we come to know the one and only true God.

To *know* someone is to know what they would do in any given circumstance, know how they feel about things, know their hopes, and know their motives and their heart. The best way to know someone that well is to walk in his shoes, if only in a minor way. Parenting a prodigal can draw us nearer to Heavenly Father, helping us to know him.

> Teaching as He has taught
> Hoping as He has hoped
> Dealing in patience as He has dealt in patience
> Forgiving as He forgives
> Showing mercy as He has been merciful
> Enduring as He has endured
> Loving as He has loved

Our foremost objective is to become as much like our Savior and our Father in Heaven as we can. "Be ye therefore perfect, even as your Father which is in heaven is perfect" (Matthew 5:48). We can transform ourselves—and we must. "The power is in them, wherein they are agents unto themselves" (D&C 58:28). The power we have is the power to lift ourselves by choosing the correct course. The path may be long and hard, with many obstacles, but that is why we are here. The pain and adversity we go through when dealing with a prodigal can be instrumental in helping us achieve this lifting process. Elder Marvin J. Ashton has said:

> We must rise by our own efforts and walk by faith. One of our greatest resources for success and happiness is doing the right thing now. All of us as God's children must be taught that meaningful growth must come from within and not from without. By so doing, we will walk in His paths, lift the arms of the weary and oppressed, give encouragement to our associates, develop individual initiative in governing ourselves, carry our crosses with dignity and purpose. (*Be of Good Cheer* [Salt Lake City: Deseret Book Co., 1987], p. 62.)

It All Depends on Our Attitude

If we do not rail, kick, and fight against it, adversity can be a great blessing. If we do fight it, then it becomes bitter for us instead of sweet. We have seen those that have become embittered because of their child's death, mean because of financial reverses, or revengeful and cruel because of humiliation at the hands of the thoughtless. Conversely, many of us have been uplifted because of the sweet spirit of a bedridden mother, the integrity of a financially poor friend, or the wise heart of a parent who has struggled with a willful child.

It is not what we have to suffer but our reaction to it that makes the difference. As the authors' mother writes: "There needs to be a decision made either to succumb to grief at the injustice life has dealt or find a way to make sense of what is happening; whether to 'pull down the shades' and resign ourselves to lives of bitterness or 'open the shades' and make our lives as fulfilling and happy as they possibly can be. Life teaches us in terms we understand; whether it be done gently or harshly does not ultimately matter. What does matter is that we heed the message." Elder Marvin J. Ashton puts it in this way: "Life can be both bitter and sweet. It is up to us to choose whether we want to reflect the voices of gloom or gladness." (*Ensign*, May 1991, p. 20.)

Truman G. Madson wrote: "The awful tragedy of this life, as of the next, is not suffering. It is 'suffering in vain.' Or worse, it is suffering that could have been the elixir of nobility, trans-forming us into a godliness beyond description, which, instead, has become the poison of bitterness and alienation." (*Eternal Man*, p. 61.)

The Book of Mormon discusses the great war the Nephites faced against the Lamanites due to the power-hungry wicked-ness of Amalickiah. It is interesting to note the difference in the attitudes of the Nephite people. It was the same adversity for all—a difficult and long war—but each person reacted to the tribulation in his or her own way. "But behold, because of the exceedingly great length of the war between the Nephites and the Lamanites many had become hardened . . . ; and many were softened because of their afflictions, insomuch that they did humble themselves before God, even in the depths of humility" (Alma 62:41).

It is in times of trial that our Heavenly Father's magnificent gift of agency can become truly meaningful in our lives. It is up to us to determine whether we will be better or worse because of our afflictions.

> Read this affirmation out loud: "I will be a different person when this problem is past. I will be a wiser, stronger, more patient person; or I will be sour, cynical, bitter, disillusioned, and angry. It all depends on what I do with this problem. Each problem can make me a better person or a worse person. It can bring me closer to God, or it can drive me away from God. It can build my faith or it can shatter my faith. It all depends on my attitude. I intend to be a better person when this problem leaves me than I was when it met me." (Robert H. Schuller, in *The Marriage Affair*, ed. J. Allan Petersen [Wheaton, Illinois: Tyndale House Publishers, 1971], p. 285.)

One of the saddest passages of scripture is that in which

Mormon describes the state of the Nephites in the last days before their destruction. They were certainly facing tribulation, the very kind of tribulation that had brought their forefathers down on their knees to repentance—but this generation would not repent:

> Thus there began to be a mourning and a lamentation in all the land because of these things, and more especially among the people of Nephi.
>
> And it came to pass that when I, Mormon, saw their lamentation and their mourning and their sorrow before the Lord, my heart did begin to rejoice within me, knowing the mercies and the long-suffering of the Lord, therefore supposing that he would be merciful unto them that they would again become a righteous people.
>
> But behold this my joy was vain, for their sorrowing was not unto repentance, because of the goodness of God; but it was rather the sorrowing of the damned, because the Lord would not always suffer them to take happiness in sin.
>
> And they did not come unto Jesus with broken hearts and contrite spirits, but they did curse God, and wish to die. Nevertheless they would struggle with the sword for their lives. (Mormon 2:11–14.)

The depth of understanding that Victor E. Frankl gained while he endured and observed many others endure one of the most horrible trials possible to suffer is worthy of our consideration. He comments that he saw men become either "saints or swine" in reaction to the concentration camp horror that had been thrust upon them.

> The way in which a man accepts his fate and all the suffering it entails, the way in which he takes up his cross, gives him ample opportunity—even under the most difficult circumstances—to add a deeper meaning to his life. It may remain brave, dignified and unselfish. Or in the bitter fight for self-preservation he may forget his human dignity and become no more than an animal. Here lies the chance for a man either to make use of or to forego

the opportunities of attaining the moral values that a difficult situation may afford him. And this decides whether he is worthy of his sufferings or not. (*Man's Search for Meaning*, p. 88.)

Frankl had had much opportunity to reflect on questions such as, Does man have no choice of action in the face of such circumstances? He gives his answer:

> We can answer these questions from experience as well as on principle. The experiences of camp life show that man does have a choice of action. There were enough examples, often of a heroic nature, which proved that apathy could be overcome, irritability suppressed. Man *can* preserve a vestige of spiritual freedom, of independence of mind, even in such terrible conditions of psychic and physical stress. . . . Fundamentally, therefore, any man can, even under such circumstances, decide what shall become of him—mentally and spiritually. (*Man's Search for Meaning*, pp. 86–87.)

If we look to the Lord in all our trials he will consecrate our afflictions to us. Lehi and Sariah had four sons when they left Jerusalem. Two more, Jacob and Joseph, were born in the desert. Jacob and Joseph were quite a bit younger than their older brothers. We are left to imagine what cruelties Laman and Lemuel may have inflicted upon them, besides the experiences on the ship, for when Lehi blessed Jacob he said: "And now, Jacob. . . . behold, in thy childhood thou has suffered afflictions and much sorrow, because of the rudeness of thy brethren. Nevertheless, Jacob . . . thou knowest the greatness of God; and he shall consecrate thine afflictions for thy gain." (2 Nephi 2:1–2.)

The Lord has told us that we have the ability to bind him by our obedience. "I, the Lord, am bound when ye do what I say; but when ye do not what I say, ye have no promise" (D&C 82:10). He has promised that there is much to gain by choosing to do things his way and much to forfeit if we do not.

For verily I say unto you, blessed is he that keepeth my commandments, whether in life or in death; and he that is faithful in tribulation, the reward of the same is greater in the kingdom of heaven.

Ye cannot behold with your natural eyes, for the present time, the design of your God concerning those things which shall come hereafter, and the glory which shall follow after much tribulation.

For after much tribulation come the blessings. (D&C 58:2–4.)

Paul, who had tried doing it his way and learned to do it the Lord's way, had this to say: "If God be for us, who can be against us?" (Romans 8:31.)

5

My Work and
My Glory

The Lord explained, "Truth is knowledge of things as they are, and as they were, and as they are to come" (D&C 93:24). Only when we put things into an eternal perspective are we able to have our lives and hearts focused on the truly consequential. This point is illustrated in a statement by Elder Melvin J. Ballard:

> If we could be conscious always of the prime purpose for which we are here it would be easier for us to reconcile ourselves. . . . I remember going into a carpet factory where they were making beautiful rugs. I approached from the seamy side. The shuttle was flying back and forth and the warp and wool were being made but there was not any design there. It was all ravelings and ends. It was just like life. When I stepped around on the other side it was another picture. It was the same operation—the same things exactly, only this was the design side. The color was blending: the figure was developing. There was not any failure there.
>
> We look at sorrows . . . and we think they are tragedies, but we are only looking at things from the seamy side. There is another side to the picture, the designer's side—God's side. And there are no blunders there. Some day we will see it. (*Crusader for Righteousness* [Salt Lake City: Bookcraft, 1966], p. 276.)

God is all-knowing and all-powerful. Our knowledge is miniscule compared to his. "For as the heavens are higher than the earth, so are my ways higher than your ways, and my thoughts than your thoughts" (Isaiah 55:9). As we broaden our focus to encompass the truths of the Lord, we know that some-day there will be no sorrow, anguish, or tears; for the Lord through his grace will remove them, and we will not remember the pain. "And God shall wipe away all tears from their eyes; and there shall be no more death, neither sorrow, nor crying, neither shall there be any more pain: for the former things are passed away" (Revelation 21:4).

The Eternal Perspective

Looking at life's challenges from an eternal perspective can shed rays of hope on a dreary scene. It can bring our souls depth and dimension when we stop looking at life from the seamy side. In the book of Moses (1:39) the Lord shows us an eternal perspective: "For behold, this is my work and my glory—to bring to pass the immortality and eternal life of man." President David O. McKay reiterated this when he said, "God's plan, God's purpose, is the perfection of humanity" (*Improvement Era*, June 1968, p. 32).

Our Father, an exalted, glorified, resurrected being, created all and does all for our edification and progress. He desires that we come back to him as joint heirs. "The whole object of the creation of this world is to exalt the intelligences that are placed upon it" (Brigham Young, in *Journal of Discourses* 7:290). A loving Father has provided us with a plan. The plan is age-less, infinite, and unchanging. "The works, and the designs, and the purposes of God cannot be frustrated, neither can they come to naught. For God doth not walk in crooked paths, neither doth he turn to the right hand nor to the left, neither doth he vary from that which he hath said, therefore his paths are straight, and his course is one eternal round. Remember, remember that it is not the work of God that is frustrated, but the work of men." (D&C 3:1–3.)

Through many divine sources we are able to receive insight about the plan of salvation and thus partly bridge the mortal gap of forgetfulness. Once we walked by sight with Father; now we must walk by faith.

We are the offspring of heavenly parents; we have been endowed with divine attributes and have their divine image imprinted upon our souls. "We are the offspring of God, born with the same faculties and powers as He possesses, capable of enlargement through the experience that we are now passing through in our second estate" (Lorenzo Snow, *Millennial Star* 56:772, 3 December 1894). Just as we know and love all our children, so are we known and loved by our Heavenly Father.

Brigham Young spoke of our knowing Him:

> I want to tell you, each and every one of you, that you are well acquainted with God our heavenly Father, or the great Eloheim. You are all well acquainted with Him, for there is not a soul of you but what has lived in His house and dwelt with Him year after year; and yet you are seeking to become acquainted with Him, when the fact is, you have merely forgotten what you did know. . . .
>
> There is not a person here to-day but what is a son or daughter of that Being. In the spirit world their spirits were first begotten and brought forth, and they lived there with their parents for ages before they came here. (In *Journal of Discourses* 4:216.)

We were in the Grand Council in Heaven and were instructed in the Creation, the Fall, and the Atonement. We learned of the world in all its beauty and vast differences that would be created for us. "All the marvels of nature are glimpses of his divine power and expressions of his love" (M. Russell Ballard, *Ensign*, May 1989, p. 59).

We understood the need for the Fall—that opposition

should be introduced into the world. We understood that this life would be a time of testing for, the Lord said: "We will make an earth whereon these may dwell; and we will prove them herewith, to see if they will do all things whatsoever the Lord their God shall command them" (Abraham 3:24–25).

We understood that, left alone, as we were tested and proved we would all fall short of the glory of God (see Romans 3:23). Therefore we would need a Savior, a Redeemer, a perfect sacrifice to atone for us. Jesus Christ, the Father's firstborn in heaven, willingly offered himself. Of this event the Father said, "Behold, my Beloved Son, which was my Beloved and Chosen from the beginning, said unto me—Father, thy will be done, and the glory be thine forever" (Moses 4:2).

We understood the Father's plan and shouted acceptance (see Job 38:7). When, for a moment, we take off our temporal glasses and behold the eternal landscape we can say, "O how great the plan of our God!" (2 Nephi 9:13.)

The Prophet Joseph Smith said, "We can never comprehend the things of God and of heaven, but by revelation" (*Teachings of the Prophet Joseph Smith*, p. 292). Just as Joseph was given the Urim and Thummim to help him translate the Book of Mormon, the Lord has provided spiritual lenses for us. With the help of the Holy Ghost, viewing the plan of salvation through spiritual lenses of faith, we can begin to fathom the intricacies of eternity.

> The gift of the Holy Spirit adapts itself to all these organs or attributes. It quickens all the intellectual faculties, increases, enlarges, expands, and purifies all the natural passions and affections, and adapts them, by the gift of wisdom, to their lawful use. It inspires, develops, cultivates, and matures all the fine-toned sympathies, joys, tastes, kindred feelings, and affections of our nature. It inspires virtue, kindness, goodness, tenderness, gentleness and charity. . . . In short, it is, as it were, marrow to the bone, joy to the heart, light to the eyes, music to the ears, and life to the whole being. (Parley P. Pratt, *Key to the Science of Theology* [Salt Lake City: Deseret Book Co., 1978], p. 61.)

Through Spiritual Lenses

The Holy Ghost is a comforter, a revelator, and the Spirit of truth. The degree to which we are influenced by the Holy Ghost determines the magnitude of our comprehension of eternity. Wrote Elder Dallin H. Oaks: "Spirituality is a lens through which we view life and a gauge by which we evaluate it. . . . Through the lens of spirituality we see all the commandments of God as invitations to blessings. Obedience and sacrifice, loyalty and love, fidelity and family, all appear in eternal perspective." (*Pure in Heart* [Salt Lake City: Bookcraft, 1988], pp. 111, 123.)

When we go through the trial brought on us by a willful and troublesome child, however, our spiritual lens can become clouded. Sometimes through guilt and frustration our perspective is dimmed. We may incorrectly assume that our problems are a form of punishment. But we also know our Father in Heaven loved his Son, our Savior, and that his suffering was not divine punishment. He made choices and exercised his agency, and in doing so descended below all things. We also exercised our agency in accepting our earthly challenges—a theme carried in the following quotation in which, basing his response on Restoration insights, Truman Madsen suggests answers a prophet might give to the mother of a blind baby.

> You and the child of your bosom counseled intimately with God the Father. Freely, fully, and with a courage that astonishes mortal imagination, you elected and prepared for this estate. The contrasts of the flesh, its risks, its terrific trials were known to you. More than that, you comprehended your actual appointed mission in this world, designed to meet your individual needs, and those who would depend upon you. Perhaps you anticipated these exact circumstances. . . .
>
> In your present nightmare a voice whips you with *why*, and *if only*, and *how long*, and *what might have been*. All that I have said may seem empty. But that fever will pass.
>
> And as it does, you will be newly sensitive to the flashes of

revelation that are your privilege in the quiet soundings of your soul. They alone can give you individual testimony of this hour's actual meaning for you. They alone can convincingly witness what seems now so utterly unbelievable. You are in the very hollow of the hand of God, a hand that will not, by your premortal request, remove you from the furnace; but will see you through it. (*Eternal Man* [Salt Lake City: Deseret Book Co., 1966], pp. 58, 60–61.)

President Spencer W. Kimball voiced similar convictions when he explained that we may be dealing now with vows we made in our premortal life. "We made vows, solemn vows, in the heavens before we came to this mortal life. . . . We made covenants. We made them before we accepted our position here on the earth." ("Be Ye Therefore Perfect," address given at University of Utah Institute Devotional, as quoted in course manual *The Life and Teachings of Jesus and His Apostles*, 1979, p. 259.) President Kimball also declared that the Lord has a perfect plan for not only our personal progression but also our children's: "God has given man knowledge of this plan. If we then accept the truth of the existence of God and his parentage then there immediately devolves upon us a responsibility to him and his children, our fellowmen. If he organized and planned the world, is it not most likely that he has made a perfect plan by which we might become closer to him and by which we might progress?" (*The Teachings of Spencer W. Kimball* [Salt Lake City: Bookcraft, 1982], p. 25.)

Some Demanding Assignments

The next few pages contain true stories of some of those who have been allowed a glimpse beyond the veil. In each of these cases it was made known that the person agreed in the premortal life to accept a demanding mission in mortality. It is important to remember, of course, that personal spiritual experiences of Church members do not determine Church doctrine and should not be used as if they did. Great comfort can be obtained from reading such stories, however, and from the knowledge that, as the Lord deems appropriate, each of us can receive comfort, insight, and guidance in our particular circumstances.

The first story is related by Dr. Carlfred Broderick, who was the stake president to the woman in the story; he is also a family counselor. He has come to call those who sacrifice for the sake of saving the living, "saviors on Mount Zion."

I first began to think in these terms as a result of counseling two women who had hard life assignments. The first had convinced her boyfriend to join the Church and one year later to marry her in the temple. Unhappily, the conversion didn't "take," and soon thereafter he returned to his worldly ways, which included all of the minor vices and several of the major ones. They had children who seemed to elect their father's lifestyle rather than their mother's. I watched this good sister struggle with her rebellious family over the years, and I am ashamed to admit that I had sometimes judged her harshly. For example, if she had asked my opinion, I could have told her before she married him that her husband-to-be was more committed to her than to the gospel. Also, I felt that she had been overly permissive with her children. In short, I self-righteously judged that if she had made better choices (as I had, for example) her life would have turned out better (as mine had, for example).

It eventually became necessary to excommunicate her husband, and in agony of spirit she asked me, her stake president, for a blessing to guide her as to what her duty was under the circumstances. In that blessing I learned a few things that even now make me burn with shame for my earlier spiritual arrogance toward that sister. The Lord told her that she was a valiant spirit in the premortal existence who had volunteered for hazardous duty on earth. Not for her was the safety of a secure marriage to an equally valiant partner. Not for her was the relative ease of rearing naturally obedient children. She had (perhaps rashly) volunteered to live her life on the front lines, as it were, of the continuing battle for men's souls. Twice, the Lord continued, she had been given the option of an honorable release from this difficult assignment. (After the blessing she confirmed this.) Twice she had been on the operating table at death's door and was given the free option of coming home or going back to face her challenging responsibilities. Twice she had squared her shoulders and returned to her difficult family. In the blessing she was told that the Lord loved her husband and her children despite their rebellious spirits and that if they were to have any chance at all it would be because of her Christlike patience and long-suffering with them.

When I took my hands off her head I bowed my head in shame, realizing that I stood in the presence of one of the Lord's great ones, truly a savior on Mount Zion.

True to her promise, she is succeeding against all odds in her mission. To everyone's surprise, her rowdy eldest son straightened out his life and went on a mission. He came back on fire with the Spirit and committed to the gospel. Her second son, who had often stated his intention of playing football instead of going on a mission, was helped by his elder brother and has also completed a successful mission and is headed for a temple marriage. Her daughters are slower to turn around, but I begin to see some softening there. Even her husband, the toughest of all, is beginning to mellow at the edges and to talk about putting his life in order (no action yet, but I am prepared to believe in miracles in this family). (Carlfred Broderick, *One Flesh, One Heart* [Salt Lake City: Deseret Book Co., 1986], pp. 50–51.)

The next story was related by a sister who was given the opportunity to "look" through the veil so that she would be able to understand that her husband had offered himself in the premortal existence as a "missionary" to his family. She received the insight that he had such strength and tenacity that he would not only be able to influence his family but also would not give up on them. One of his family members who has been influenced by him said, "You wouldn't dare not have a testimony around Sam."

My husband courted me while we were in college; consequently, I had no real opportunity to meet his family before our marriage. In the months following our marriage I was to find out that he came from a family plagued with problems and Church inactivity. Coincidentally, a few years later a close friend of mine married into a lovely, active LDS family. In fact, her new father-in-law held a high Church leadership position. Naturally, she was thrilled and humbled to be included in such an exemplary family.

Her newfound joy touched off something deep within me that I had been hiding, even from myself. I had been taught, as a young girl, that spirits were sent to families based on their pre-earth valiancy. Also, that the truly righteous spirits were sent to active LDS families to be given the best opportunity for growth. All of these early teachings now exploded in my thoughts: What, then, did this make of my husband? Did his family situation mean I had married someone who had not been valiant in the premortal existence? I started to pray about this matter in great earnestness because I was confused and hurt.

A few days later, I received an answer. It came just as Joseph Smith described, in a burst of "pure intelligence" flowing through me. I was given to understand that in the premortal existence my husband had been a spirit of great valiancy, and that he could have gone to any fine LDS family. It was made clear to me that the choice had been his. He had agreed to be born to this particular family so that he could be a missionary to them. It has been many years since the Spirit enlightened me about one of the earthly missions of my husband. Through sheer strength of will, caring, and example, I have seen my husband pull in sisters, brothers, uncles, and aunts. How many have been redeemed because of his influence I cannot count. What a blessing it is to have the Holy Ghost teach us the truth of things as they really are!

Who knows but what we ourselves, or some other struggling parent, accepted a heavy assignment? Regardless, we need to be supportive of parents we know who are doing their best, and appreciate that the Lord's view may be different from ours. "Ye cannot behold with your natural eyes, for the present time, the design of your God concerning those things which shall come hereafter, and the glory which shall follow after much tribulation" (D&C 58:3).

My sister is a wonderful person with truly fine and spiritual children. She had a hard time understanding why I had several children who were of a more rebellious nature. Though she was never unkind, she was somewhat patronizing at times.

One day she came to see me, apparently preoccupied with something. She explained to me that she had dreamed of the premortal existence. In the dream, she and I were standing together, and she was given to understand that we were choosing the spirits that would be our earthly children. There was a "coordinator" standing next to us who was telling us something about each spirit as he or she passed: "This first one will be a fine young man—a real asset to his family; this next one, though, will be strong-willed and hard to reach; now, here is a spirit that will be a joy in every way; this one will be a real struggle; this girl coming along will have a sweet nature; but the girl behind her will challenge the most patient parent." Spirit after spirit passed in this way.

My sister said to me with tears in her eyes: "I did not take any of the difficult ones. But you did. All the spirits you took were challenges."

A close family relationship can be one of the ways the Lord helps to bring back his children. Often when we have been struggling with someone we love very much, and as the battle lasts day after day and year after year, we lose sight of the true value of these precious loved ones.

My brother Tom and I had been very close as children, so it was a great source of grief to me when he chose to take a worldly path. I talked with him, reasoned with him, and loved him; all to no avail. He insisted on clinging to his profane values.

It was so painful for me to deal with him that I had about decided to let him go his own way. Just as I reached the lowest point of my hopelessness toward him, my understanding was opened and I "saw" him from a distant viewpoint. I somehow understood that in the premortal existence he had been a valiant fighter on the side of right and a terrible enemy to Lucifer. It became clear to my understanding that Satan would fight very hard to keep him because if Tom ever got loose from him and joined the Lord's side he would be a terrible opponent and do much damage to Satan's kingdom.

We have been given the privilege of being a parent in these latter days to help in the winding-up scene. It can be a difficult role, but one with many blessings and rewards if we are willing to seek the Lord. It has been said that a mother's love can be the closest to the Savior's love. But to be blessed with either a father or a mother who loves us and prays for us can be one of the greatest blessings of life.

> I had always honored my mother because she had raised her children, as best she knew how, by the promptings of the Spirit. I knew that she had taught me many things that I had passed on to my own family. But it was when I was having some real difficulties with one of my own children that I came to realize just how blessed I had been to be her daughter.
>
> My brothers and I were raised in the sixties, when so much was changing in the world—particularly concerning drugs and morals. A few of us fell prey to the pressure of the day. Mother worked and struggled and loved. The one thing she did not do was give up on any one of us. So when it came time for me to go through my own difficulties with my children, I applied much of what I had learned from her.
>
> One day, as I was praying, I understood, as I had never really understood before, the heavenly wisdom that had guided our family through those treacherous years. I felt that my brothers and I had been sent to this mother because our Heavenly Father knew that by her very nature she would not let go of us, but would fight tenaciously for us and our salvation. She won, you know, and so will I.

The Lord depends on each of us. He will strengthen and support us. "Let us not be weary in well doing: for in due season we shall reap, if we faint not" (Galatians 6:9).

It can become so easy to faint and temporarily lose heart. The outrageous statements your child makes, the accusations toward every member of the family, the hateful words—all of this and more can cause us to become discouraged. We can easily lose our eternal perspective when the battle goes on year after year. Satan will use every possible influence to thwart our parental assignment and to stop us from moving closer to the

Lord. Elder Heber C. Kimball reported these words of Joseph Smith's: "The nearer a person approaches the Lord, a greater power will be manifested by the adversary to prevent the accomplishments of His purposes" (in Orson F. Whitney, *Life of Heber C. Kimball* [Salt Lake City: Bookcraft, 1973], p. 132). The harder we try to succeed, the more Satan will try to discourage and defeat us. He will use every weakness against us in his attack.

If to our marriage we have brought differences in parenting styles, or personal wounds that have not healed, or past mistakes that can be magnified, or scars of varying kinds, Satan will use all this against us. Then our struggles may become a dual conflict: the challenges we face with our child, and our own inner conflicts and feelings of inadequacy. But Elder Howard W. Hunter has reminded us: "We should never let Satan fool us into thinking that all is lost. Let us take pride in the good and right things we have done; reject and cast out of our lives those things that are wrong; look to the Lord for forgiveness, strength, and comfort; and then move onward." (*Ensign*, November 1983, p. 65.)

We must remember what the Lord has told us about our children. We need to look with an eternal view; we need to see the value the Lord has placed upon them and the trust the Lord has in their ability to make it through the trials of the last days. Though they may fall and be wounded in battle, there is every reason to hope and believe that they will recover their former valiancy and will survive the great tests. In the 1990 Church pamphlet called *For the Strength of Youth* (page 3), the First Presidency state: "You are not just ordinary young men and women. You are choice spirits who have been held in reserve to come forth in this day when the temptations, responsibilities, and opportunities are the very greatest. . . . God loves you as He loves each and every one of His children. His desire, purpose, and glory is to have you return to Him. . . . Your Father in Heaven is mindful of you."

Also, in a message by President Ezra Taft Benson he told the young women: "You have been born at this time for a sacred and glorious purpose. It is not by chance that you have been reserved to come to earth in this last dispensation of the fulness of times. Your birth at this particular time was foreordained in the eternities." (*Come, Listen to a Prophet's Voice* [Salt Lake City: Deseret Book Co., 1990], p. 14.)

As we read these quotations, we may be able to intellectually say, "That's true! That's right!" But as we witness our children going through the degradation and filth, we as loving parents reach down and try to help them. When we do this, some of that filth may splatter on us and get into our eyes. Our view can become distorted and cloudy and we may become blinded and lose our eternal sight. We see the filth of their lives today and their lost potential. We question the Lord, ourselves, and life, wondering if these quotations apply to our child. If so, why is he making these dreadful choices? We look at our child through our narrow, finite scope. We forget how long the Lord's arms are, how deep his reach is, and how purifying the Savior's atonement is. God sees things from an eternal aspect. In order to restore our hope, and give us an eternal perspective, we must be cleansed by the Savior's purifying blood.

> *As I saw this sweet, loving daughter who had such wonderful potential make one foolish choice after another my heart began to ache for her. We would have long discussions and progress would be made, and I would find myself having such hopes. Then she would go back and move deeper into the pit she had dug for herself. Finally, she moved out of our home to be able to freely live the style of degradation she had chosen for herself. Even then, she would come back home and change for a time, and hope would begin to build within me again, but it would be quickly shattered as she would go back.*
>
> *The scripture began to run through my mind, "The dog is turned to his own vomit again," and I would weep in anguish. I would weep over the life and potential she was squandering and throwing away. I would weep at the mental pictures I saw of a life of degradation instead of joy and peace. I would weep because I would know that someday she would have to stand before the Lord to give an accounting; and I*

knew the suffering and pain that she would go through as she recognized the waste.

As I was pondering, anguishing, and praying about her, a wonderful feeling of knowledge and understanding came over me. I understood from the purest form of intelligence that my daughter and so many others like her could be of great value, that God would consecrate her experience to his service, that she could become a child of transition, a pivotal point. She would have invaluable experience to offer, much as recovered alcoholics can reach other alcoholics. She would be qualified to stand at the gates of hell and be a light to help those who are lost in darkness, and pilot them back home. Standing as a sentinel at that gate, she could also block the entrance of so many youth who are willingly rushing toward it. She would have knowledge, understanding, and credibility as to what was beyond the gate.

Sweet comfort entered my soul to know that God was aware of her, that he loved her, that she was not lost to him, and that she could have a place in his kingdom. I have lived to see the fruition of the Lord's comforting reassurance. My daughter has valiantly come back and is so grateful for the love and mercy of the Lord. Time and time again she has been called to work with the youth.

As we look at our children we need to see them through the only clear lenses—from the eternal perspective. We will then be able to make correct decisions about our lives and our children's welfare. As President Spencer W. Kimball said: "The more clearly we see eternity, the more obvious it becomes that the Lord's work in which we are engaged is one vast and grand work with striking similarities on each side of the veil. . . . If we live in such a way that the considerations of eternity press upon us, we will make better decisions." (*The Teachings of Spencer W. Kimball*, p. 25.)

God's purposes will go forth. We must decide whether we are going forward with him. His grand work cannot be stopped, for he has declared: "How long can rolling waters remain impure? What power shall stay the heavens? As well might man stretch forth his puny arm to stop the Missouri river in its decreed course, or to turn it up stream, as to hinder the Almighty from pouring down knowledge from heaven upon the heads of the Latter-day Saints." (D&C 121:33.)

The Lord has given each of us an opportunity to receive his own personal revelation and glimpse into the eternities. A patriarchal blessing is a revelation to the person who has received it and the blessings it contains are predicated upon righteous living. Through a patriarchal blessing we may know our strengths and weaknesses. We can receive guidance, counsel, and comfort. We can realize that the Lord has made eternal covenants with us and will be there throughout our trials and tribulations. A patriarchal blessing can be a glimpse into our eternal possibilities; and if our children have received their blessings, reading them can remind us of *their* eternal possibilities. We will see the valiancy of their spirits and have hope in the Savior's redeeming atonement. We will remember that they will again be drawn back to him.

Following marriage and graduation, we settled down far from home and relatives. Our isolation and independence was enjoyable at first, but in time we longed for a more frequent association with our families. Eventually this led us to take many long trips to visit family and friends. With little money to spare, we would pack up the old car and six kids and head out on the long, long road.

In fact, the only reason we put ourselves through this disagreeable experience was because we were going home. The children rarely played the games we prepared for them; they preferred "space wars," the battle of who is sitting in my space and breathing my air; and "why can't I sit by the window?" Then there was "car tag," which usually didn't stop until Father's long, hairy arm reached into the back seat to grab anyone he could get. Well, you get the picture: we were crowded; there was fighting, car sickness, squalling babies, boredom, and only occasionally was there something interesting to see along the vast, barren desert roads.

It's interesting that when I think back on those trips it is with sweet nostalgia. I don't remember the hot weather, the arguing, or how miserable the trip seemed. I do remember the wonderful memories of the stays in California, how much fun we had when we got there, and the

excitement when we would reach the landmarks that signaled we were
close to home. Fondest of all are the memories of knocking on Mom's
front door and the hugs at the end of the road—we were home.

Life is a journey home. Much of the time it is tedious, trying, and laborious; occasionally it is joyous, and sometimes it is
tragic. Through it all, no matter what we encounter—bad
weather, poor road conditions, car trouble, or difficult family situations—this is still our journey home. When all things have
been considered the only issue is, Did we get home? We, too,
have parents—heavenly parents—waiting for us to come up
past the landmarks.

He is the Father of our spirits; and if we could know, understand, and do His will, every soul would be prepared to return
back into His presence. And when they get there, they would see
that they had formerly lived there for ages, that they had previously been acquainted with every nook and corner, with the
palaces, walks, and gardens; and they would embrace their Father, and He would embrace them and say, "My son, my daughter,
I have you again;" and the child would say, "O my Father, my Father, I am here again." (Brigham Young, in *Journal of Discourses*
4:268.)

As we struggle to rescue our children from the murky mists,
we tend to forget that we are all children of our Father in
Heaven, that he has a plan, and that his purpose will go forth.
He is never thwarted. He has given us the Light of the World,
Jesus Christ, to guide us as we walk through this cloud of dark-
ness. We must always remember our Father's main purpose:
"This is my work and my glory—to bring to pass the immortal-
ity and eternal life of man" (Moses 1:39).

6

They Will Return

Parents of a prodigal who are living through their darkest moment, who have seen all that they cherish go down into the abyss of despair, may take comfort from these three words: They will return. In the general conference of April 1929, Elder Orson F. Whitney said:

> The Prophet Joseph Smith declared—and he never taught more comforting doctrine—that the eternal sealings of faithful parents and the divine promises made to them for valiant service in the Cause of Truth, would save not only themselves, but likewise their posterity.
>
> Though some of the sheep may wander, the eye of the Shepherd is upon them, and sooner or later they will feel the tentacles of Divine Providence reaching out after them and drawing them back to the fold. Either in this life or the life to come, they will return.
>
> They will have to pay their debt to justice; they will suffer for their sins; and may tread a thorny path; but if it leads them at last, like the penitent Prodigal, to a loving and forgiving father's heart and home, the painful experience will not have been in vain. Pray for your careless and disobedient children; hold on to them with your faith. Hope on, trust on, till you see the salvation of God. (CR, April 1929, p. 110.)

What a wonderful statement of hope! What a transcendent gift to have a God of hope and a Savior of mercy! It is the responsibility of parents to prayerfully inquire of the Lord to understand how, where, and under what circumstances the statement "faithful parents . . . would save . . . their posterity" will be fulfilled. The Savior will be the judge. Our children may be involved in varying degrees of sin, but the Lord will take into account the totality of circumstances and the level of accountability of each child.

> Sin is the transgression of divine law, as made known through the conscience or by revelation. A man sins when he violates his conscience, going contrary to light and knowledge—not the light and knowledge that has come to his neighbor, but that which has come to himself. He sins when he does the opposite of what he knows to be right. Up to that point he only blunders. One may suffer painful consequences for only blundering, but he cannot commit sin unless he knows better than to do the thing in which the sin consists. One must have a conscience before he can violate it. (Orson F. Whitney, *Saturday Night Thoughts*, p. 239.)

The Savior will not judge children by the light and knowledge of the parents; nor will he judge according to what we as parents believe about the spiritual condition of our children. The details of judgment are strictly in the hands of the Lord. We should not dabble in speculation about it—even with our flesh-and-blood offspring. On the matter of judgment the Prophet Joseph Smith taught:

> While one portion of the human race is judging and condemning the other without mercy, the Great Parent of the universe looks upon the whole of the human family with a fatherly care and paternal regard. . . . He is a wise Lawgiver, and will judge all men, not according to the narrow, contracted notions of men, but, "according to the deeds done in the body whether they be good or evil". . . . We need not doubt the wisdom and intelligence of the Great Jehovah; He will award judgment or mercy to

all. . . . according to their several deserts, their means of obtaining intelligence, the laws by which they are governed, the facilities afforded them of obtaining correct information, and His inscrutable designs in relation to the human family; and when the designs of God shall be made manifest, and the curtain of futurity be withdrawn, we shall all of us eventually have to confess that the Judge of all the earth has done right. (*Teachings of the Prophet Joseph Smith*, sel. Joseph Fielding Smith [Salt Lake City: Deseret Book Co., 1938], p. 218.)

The Lord is squarely on our side; he will fight our battles and will sustain us. We must be anchored in him for our strength and support. Elder Paul H. Dunn recounts the reassuring story of Elisha in 2 Kings.

Elisha, the prophet, had every reason to be depressed. He had successfully helped the king of Israel avoid the traps laid for him and his people by the king of Syria, but now Elisha was in deep trouble himself. The king of Syria had just arrived to take revenge.

"Therefore sent he thither horses, and chariots, and a great host: and they came by night, and compassed the city about.

"And when the servant of the man of God was risen early, and gone forth, behold, an host compassed the city both with horses and chariots. And his servant said unto him, Alas, my master! how shall we do?" (2 Kings 6:14–15.)

Elisha and a boy against the Syrian army! I think if I had been that boy I would not only have asked, "How shall we do?" but, in fact, would have asked several other questions, such as, "Are you sure we are doing the right thing?" or "Which way is the quickest exit?" But note:

"And he answered, Fear not: for they that be with us are more than they that be with them.

"And Elisha prayed, and said, Lord, I pray thee, open his eyes, that he may see. And the Lord opened the eyes of the young man; and he saw: and, behold, the mountain was full of horses and chariots of fire round about Elisha." (2 Kings 6:16–17.)

As you may recall, Elisha and the boy were victorious.

Now, I assure you that the same heavenly hosts are available
to us in our day. They come to our rescue just as speedily as they
did for Elisha and his servant. They can smite depression and despair. They can strike down discouragement and fear. They are
available twenty-four hours a day, seven days a week. When we
do all we can, when we have exhausted all our resources, and
when we humble ourselves and seek His help, it will be there. I
know from personal, sacred experiences that heavenly powers
can be released in our behalf. It has been true for me and it is true
for all. It is an eternally true principle. (*Variable Clouds, Occa-
sional Rain, with a Promise of Sunshine* [Salt Lake City: Bookcraft,
1986], pp. 7–8.)

The scriptures declare, "If God be for us, who can be against
us?" (Romans 8:31.) President Ezra Taft Benson also testified
that our Heavenly Father is on our side and that heavenly hosts
yearn for our victory: "God loves us. He's watching us, he wants
us to succeed, and we'll know someday that he has not left one
thing undone for the eternal welfare of each of us. If we only
knew it, there are heavenly hosts pulling for us—friends in
heaven that we can't remember now, who yearn for our victory."
(*Ensign*, July 1975, p. 63.)

The Apostle Paul speaks of our inability to see beyond this
earthly existence and realize that God is over all. One day we
will see "face to face" and know, but for now we need to abide
in, "faith, hope, charity" (1 Corinthians 13:12, 13). Faith, hope,
and charity are interwoven. They are part of the same flower.
Every plant needs light, water, soil, and air in order to live and
grow. Christ is our light; he is our living water; he is our rock of
salvation, the soil in which we plant ourselves deep. He is our
life.

Faith

The Apostle Paul tells us that faith is "the substance of
things hoped for, the evidence of things not seen" (Hebrews

11:1). Paul uses examples of faith, citing Abel, Enoch, Abraham, Joseph, Moses, and other men of great faith. In each instance he starts by saying, "By faith . . ." and goes on to explain what was done by the person through faith. From this we can assume that the Lord expects us to show our faith through certain actions so that we may obtain the blessings associated with the act of faith. Moroni, who wrote a chapter very much like Paul's, tells us: "I would show unto the world that faith is things which are hoped for and not seen; wherefore, dispute not because ye see not, for ye receive no witness until after the trial of your faith" (Ether 12:6).

Magnificent rewards are applied to the promises of faith: "And as surely as Christ liveth he spake these words unto our fathers, saying: Whatsoever thing ye shall ask the Father in my name, which is good, in faith believing that ye shall receive, behold, it shall be done unto you. Wherefore, my beloved brethren, have miracles ceased? . . . They who have faith in him will cleave unto every good thing." (Moroni 7:26–28.)

Christ promises us that if we will exercise faith, nothing shall be impossible for us. "For verily I say unto you, If ye have faith as a grain of mustard seed, ye shall say unto this mountain, Remove hence to yonder place; and it shall remove; and nothing shall be impossible unto you" (Matthew 17:20).

Particular conditions require commensurate acts of faith. God gave understanding to Noah that the world was to be flooded; the act of faith was to build an ark. God promised an old woman that a child of promise was to be born from her body; the act of faith was to prepare for pregnancy and childbirth. It was an act of faith to walk through the middle of the Red Sea on dry land (see Hebrews 11). Likewise, if we have a son or daughter who is completely out of control, an act of faith for us would be to bend our knees, receive an answer from the Lord, and trust in him no matter how long it seems to take for our child to return.

The wisdom of the ages supports the belief that there will come a point in the lives of prodigals when they will tire of themselves in that state and of living with the consequences of their detrimental choices. There will come a time when they can no longer stomach the feast of worldliness. Brigham Young explained: "Some few of those who give rein to their wild and foolish notions, and seemingly give themselves up to destruction, will meet hard times: suffering and trouble will arrest them in their wild career, and then they will begin to inquire after their friends. They will seek those whose bosoms are filled with compassion and goodwill towards them, will cease their follies, and their friends will rejoice over them in their efforts to become good and wise. Do not be discouraged." (In *Journal of Discourses* 7:336.)

When POWs return from war they are usually not much more than skin and bones. But as they are allowed to return to their homes and their usual life-style an interesting phenomenon occurs. Those who were previously thin remain thin, but those who were heavy or overweight before their POW experience regain their former weight. That is, the bodies return to just about the same physical size as before the experience. The nutrition experts call this weight per individual a "set point." They explain that the body has a tendency to restore itself to its natural or usual state.

Our spirit too is like that. That is, we have a set point that naturally gravitates toward the spiritual. President David O. McKay wrote: "Man is a spiritual being, a soul, and at some period of his life everyone is possessed with an irresistible desire to know his relationship to the Infinite. . . . There is something within him that urges him to rise above himself. . . . There is in man a spiritual longing, a desire for spiritual communion which attends and which may at all times lift him from that which is physical and sensual to the realm of spirituality." (*Secrets of a Happy Life*, comp. Llewelyn R. McKay [Salt Lake City: Bookcraft, 1967], p. 116.)

Parents who have done all they can to bring up their child in righteousness have reinforced the set point within their child. To use a computer analogy, it is simpler to retrieve information that is already stored in memory than to enter new information. Similarly, if a child has been taught correct principles, sin and corruption will not totally erase them regardless of present circumstances. In the words of President Spencer W. Kimball:

> I have sometimes seen children of good families rebel, resist, stray, sin, and even actually fight God. In this they bring sorrow to their parents, who have done their best to set in movement a current and to teach and live as examples. But I have repeatedly seen many of these same children, after years of wandering, mellow, realize what they have been missing, repent, and make great contribution to the spiritual life of their community. The reason I believe this can take place is that, despite all the adverse winds to which these people have been subjected, they have been influenced still more, and much more than they realized, by the current of life in the homes in which they were reared. When, in later years, they feel a longing to recreate in their own families the same atmosphere they enjoyed as children, they are likely to turn to the faith that gave meaning to their parents' lives. (*The Teachings of Spencer W. Kimball* [Salt Lake City: Bookcraft, 1982], p. 335.)

An oft-quoted scripture concerning the hope and assurance of the return of a prodigal states: "Train up a child in the way he should go: and when he is old, he will not depart from it" (Proverbs 22:6). This maxim is conditional in at least two ways: the child must be trained in correct principles; and long-suffering may be required on the parents' part, because the return may not come quickly. However, the assurance is that eventually "he will not depart from [the teachings]." He will return.

In Luke chapter 15 Jesus teaches three parables that have application to those children who become lost. These three parables have one basic theme: the lost one returns. When the lost sheep wanders off, the shepherd will go after him. When the coin is lost through carelessness, the owner will call in all resources and other stewards until it is found. The prodigal who openly rebels will be tutored through natural consequences of adversity and seek the refuge of home. The Savior has said: "My sheep hear my voice, and I know them, and they follow me. . . . My Father, which gave them me, is greater than all; and no man is able to pluck them out of my Father's hand. I and my Father are one." (John 10:27, 29–30.) In these three parables we see the lengths to which the Savior will go to find his sheep, and the rejoicing of the Father.

The parable of the prodigal son is possibly the most applicable to our situation: a good father, a righteous and loving father, loses one of his sons. Although the son leaves home against his father's wishes, he is aware of his father's virtue and it is the memory of that goodness and love that he depends on when he finally returns. This highly esteemed parable is characteristic of the drama experienced by grieving latter-day parents. The prodigal's return in particular evokes the same response as it always did: "For this my son was dead, and is alive again; he was lost, and is found" (Luke 15:24).

> *Shawn had been a sickly child, so Mother got in the habit of indulging him. As he grew older, she continued doting over him. The trouble started to show when Shawn was about fourteen. It started out slowly at first, so Mom was able to pretend it wasn't happening. Finally, though, even Mom had to recognize how bad it had become.*
>
> *He started with drugs and then devil worship. He claims he used to have two evil spirits in his room at all times. He even maintains that he saw Satan himself. He says that at one point Satan offered him anything he wanted in return for his soul. Whether it really happened or he just imagined it, the incident scared Shawn so badly he quit taking drugs and stopped devil worshipping. However, he continued to drink and be immoral. He drifted in and out of a few marriages. He came to church for a while, but got discouraged and went back to his old life. Because he had been involved in an abortion and in devil worship, he felt he had done too much to ever be forgiven.*
>
> *Throughout all these years, the family went up and down in their hope for Shawn's return. But Mother never gave up hoping nor stopped loving him. There were three things she never failed to do for*

him: *She fasted and prayed constantly. She put his name in the temple regularly. She was a true lady of charity to everyone.*

Finally, Shawn began his slow return. He met a nice girl and she has been wonderful for him. He's been able to go to the temple with this wife. He's active and has a Church calling. The only one who's not surprised is Mom.

Brigham Young corroborated the assurance related earlier in this chapter about faithful parents saving their posterity. "Parents—you who continue to live the life of true Christians, and are filled with faith, virtue, and good works, I promise you, in the name of Israel's God, that you will have your children, and no power can rob you of them. . . . If they go to hell, you will have the privilege of dragging them from there, if you are faithful." (In *Journal of Discourses* 7:336.)

In connection with these promises the prophets have stressed the qualifying relevance of temple sealings. Elder Boyd K. Packer referred to the ordinance of sealing children to their parents as "the binding ties." He asserted, "When parents keep the covenants they have made at the altar of the temple, their children will be forever bound to them." (*Ensign*, May 1992, p. 68.) Brigham Young amplifies this concept further:

> Let the father and mother, who are members of this Church and kingdom, take a righteous course, and strive with all their might never to do a wrong, but to do good all their lives; if they have one child or one hundred children, if they conduct themselves towards them as they should, binding them to the Lord by their faith and prayers, I care not where those children go, they are bound up to their parents by an everlasting tie, and no power of earth or hell can separate them from their parents in eternity; they will return again to the fountain from whence they sprang. (In Joseph Fielding Smith, *Doctrines of Salvation*, comp. Bruce R. McConkie, 3 vols. [Salt Lake City: Bookcraft, 1954–56], 2:90–91.)

Elder James E. Faust also speaks of the covenants and divine promises made in the temple concerning our children:

There are some great spiritual promises which may help faithful parents in this church. Children of eternal sealings may have
visited upon them the divine promises made to their valiant fore-
bears who nobly kept their covenants. Covenants remembered by
parents will be remembered by God. The children may thus become the beneficiaries and inheritors of these great covenants
and promises. This is because they are the children of the
covenant. (*Ensign,* November 1990, p. 35.)

Hope

Christ's atonement is the focal point of all humanity. It is
the greatest act of charity of all time, giving mankind hope
through infinite atonement. As Moroni explains, "ye shall have
hope through the atonement of Christ and the power of his resurrection, to be raised unto life eternal, and this because of your
faith in him according to the promise" (Moroni 7:41).

Alma explains that justice demands full payment and must
be satisfied. This satisfaction comes through the atonement of
Jesus Christ, in which he paid for the sins of all mankind. With
the demands of justice thus satisfied, the Lord can extend mercy
to the repentant. Our hope, therefore, is in Christ and his mercy.

Mercy is one of the attributes of God. "Mercy is the very
essence of the gospel of Jesus Christ" (Gordon B. Hinckley, *Ensign,* May 1990, p. 69). The scriptures speak repeatedly of a God
of mercy, "tender mercy," "abundant mercy," and "infinite
mercy" (see James 5:11; Peter 1:3; Mosiah 28:4). Elder Orson F.
Whitney spoke of mercy to the wayward.

> You parents of the willful and the wayward: Don't give them
> up. Don't cast them off. They are not utterly lost. The Shepherd
> will find his sheep. They were his before they were yours—long
> before he entrusted them to your care; and you cannot begin to
> love them as he loves them. They have but strayed in ignorance
> from the Path of Right, and God is merciful to ignorance. Only
> the fullness of knowledge brings the fullness of accountability.

Our Heavenly Father is far more merciful, infinitely more chari-
table, than even the best of his servants, and the Everlasting
Gospel is mightier in power to save than our narrow finite minds
can comprehend. (CR, April 1929, p. 110.)

Be assured that our Father with his Only Begotten Son will
extend every mercy possible to your child. Moreover, he has
promised that he can make everything all right. "And he said
unto me, My grace is sufficient for thee: for my strength is made
perfect in weakness. Most gladly therefore will I rather glory in
my infirmities, that the power of Christ may rest upon me." (2
Corinthians 12:9.) As Ted Gibbons stood in the Garden of
Gethsemane these were his thoughts:

> Blood had been spilled in this place. The best blood ever shed
> fell here in response to a suffering which caused even the Son of
> God to tremble and shrink. And some of that blood was spilled
> for me. Some of that suffering was a gift to me. I knew Christ had
> paid for the sins of men. But standing there, in that holy place, I
> learned that he had paid for my sins. The Sanhedrin and the
> temple guard brought him to judgment and to the Antonia
> Fortress. Pilate brought him to the cross. But I brought him to
> Gethsemane—my choices, my life, my sins. (Ted Gibbons, *Mis-
> ery and Joy* [Orem, Utah: Keepsake Publishing, 1991], p. 10.)

In discussing the infinite nature of the Atonement, Elder
Neal A. Maxwell wrote:

> Thus the Atonement *may* reach into the universe—even as
> its blessings and redemptive powers reach into the small universe
> of each individual's suffering. How infinite indeed! . . . That
> blood in each and every pore further symbolizes infiniteness.
>
> Knowing as we do that before the scourging and crucifixion
> Jesus bled at every pore in Gethsemane, how red His raiment
> must have been then, how crimson His cloak!
>
> No wonder that, in one of His appearances—when He comes
> in power and glory—Christ will come in red attire (D&C
> 133:48), thereby not only signifying the winepress of wrath but

also bringing to our remembrance how He suffered, for each of us, in Gethsemane and on Calvary! (*Not My Will, But Thine* [Salt Lake City: Bookcraft, 1988], pp. 52–53.)

How great and glorious is the plan of our God! Heavenly Father knew he was sending his spirits down to an imperfect life on earth. He knew there would be foolish parents, clumsy teachers, and tired and overworked Church leaders. He knew that his spirit children were not going to have their tutoring done always by perfect hands. Many mentors along the way would make mistakes with his children and perhaps even facilitate their wrongdoing. That is one of the reasons why our wise Father prepared a Savior. "For God so loved the world, that he gave his only begotten Son, that whosoever believeth in him should not perish, but have everlasting life. For God sent not his Son into the world to condemn the world; but that the world through him might be saved." (John 3:16–17.)

At a very early age I became aware of my spiritual strengths, my gifts, and the reason I was here. When I was twelve, I had a witness of Jesus Christ and his love for me. The experience was to carry me through the terrible difficulties that would later befall me.

I was very active in my ward, and at school; I was editor of the school newspaper, was in all the honors classes, and my ambition was to go on to college and be a lawyer. But when I was sixteen my world crashed! My father began molesting me. There are not words to describe how shattering that experience is.

I told my mother, but she did not believe me. So I lost both parents. Not through death, though surely that must be a more merciful way to lose your parents; then you at least have the assurance of their love and carry the memory of trust in them. I had nothing. I had no family. I had no love. I had no one. I even turned to the bishop, but that was so many years ago when these things were not understood. He tried to help but was told by my father to stop meddling in family affairs. When I lost even the help of the bishop the last hope died within me. I had no feeling, no emotions; I was empty and felt like no one and nothing.

I left home, and for a while I lived in my car. To support myself I took a job in a foster home, where for two years I slept in the basement in the furnace room. I dated a man that was abusive, but his family was good to me. As I look back on it now, I realize I married him because of my intense hunger for a family. I stayed in the marriage for about five years. I left because his abuse became so severe that I feared for my life. Because my self-esteem was completely gone, I continued to date abusive men—I thought I deserved no better. This went on for over three more years.

Then the Lord sent me a friend, a visiting teacher. The Relief Society president did not know me, because I was not active, but she felt strongly that Carol needed to be my visiting teacher. We both had a feeling of recognition and became instant friends. Carol had worked through some similar problems herself and had studied it out. She seemed to know just the scriptures I could read to get answers. She counseled me about prayer; we talked about everything. She told me to send for my patriarchal blessing. She advised me to see the bishop and get the past cleared up.

As I began to do all of this, the feelings of love from my Savior returned. On more than one occasion as I struggled through my pain and cried out to the Lord, I could feel his arms of love hold me and whisper peace to my soul. I know that Christ loves me. He has taken my pain and sorrow and given me strength, peace, and joy. Each day I grow stronger and stronger and feel closer and closer to the Lord. I'm so grateful to know that I am a daughter of God and that he loves me.

As abused children, neglected spouses, crime victims, maligned individuals, or parents of prodigals, we receive injuries: deep, open wounds with raw nerve endings. The atonement of Jesus Christ is a divine ointment and protective cream, our balm of Gilead. As we take upon us his name, we receive his succoring and healing. Indeed, we choose to put on his very countenance—"Have ye received his image in your countenances?" Alma asked. (Alma 5:14.) As we embrace the Atonement in our lives it heals, protects, soothes, and acts as a barrier against new injuries, for Jesus Christ has taken upon himself the pain, suffering, infirmities, and sickness we incur (see Alma

7:11–12). In like manner, as a prodigal returns and rebuilds his or her testimony, so too will these blessings of the Atonement and the healing balm cover the pain of past wounds.

His grace takes care of it all; his "grace is sufficient" (Ether 12:27). This means that all will be made right. This does not mean that his Atonement will simply do a repair job. No, his grace will make everything as new. That is the beauty of the plan of salvation. Father can send his beloved spirits down to imperfect situations because the Atonement is so all-encompassing and complete. His grace will cover everyone's mistakes: yours, mine, and theirs; foolhardy parents, and well-meaning leaders. Our stubborn youngsters, instead of having to suffer forever for their mistakes, can have their sins washed white as snow. "Come now, and let us reason together, saith the Lord: though your sins be as scarlet, they shall be as white as snow; though they be red like crimson, they shall be as wool" (Isaiah 1:18).

Elder Boyd K. Packer has commented: "I know of no sins connected with the moral standard for which we cannot be forgiven. I do not exempt abortion." (*Ensign*, May 1992, p. 68.) He goes on to add: "The formula is stated in forty words: 'Behold, he who has repented of his sins, the same is forgiven, and I the Lord, remember them no more. By this may ye know if a man repenteth of his sins—behold, he will confess them and forsake them.' (D&C 58:42–43.)" There is much to hope for. We have been promised that our children will return and our Savior has provided the gracious door for that return.

Notwithstanding the quick-fix demands of this instant society of ours, experience indicates that resuscitating the spiritually dying usually requires an abundance of time. God's time is not our time, and only he knows when the time is right. God likens Israel to an olive tree. It takes at least twenty years of nurturing and caring before an olive tree starts to produce. Sometimes it even takes them thirty to forty years before they bear fruit. In the meantime, the orchard growers continue to nurture, dig about, weed, and pluck out the wild branches.

Once it is finally producing good fruit, it is virtually indestructible. You can cut it down and it will still send up new shoots. It can go without water for a long time because its roots are so deep. Graft in wild branches and the tree will tame them. So it is that the Lord compares his Israel with the olive tree. The lesson we must learn is that the business of raising offspring takes time and patience. Elder Richard G. Scott tenderly explains:

> Your life is filled with anguish, pain, and, at times, despair. I will tell you how you can be comforted by the Lord.
>
> First, you must recognize two foundation principles:
>
> 1. While there are many things you can do to help a loved one in need, there are some things that must be done by the Lord.
>
> 2. Also, no enduring improvement can occur without righteous exercise of agency. Do not attempt to override agency. The Lord himself would not do that. Forced obedience yields no blessings (see D&C 58:26–33). (*Ensign*, May 1988, p. 60.)

God has his timetable, we have ours, and our children have theirs. We cannot push them into our timetable; we cannot force them to repent. This is contrary to divine law. During this crisis, we must learn and have faith in other divine laws by which the Lord operates. We must look with hope to the mercy in Christ. "We have a hope in Christ here and now. He died for our sins. Because of him and his gospel, our sins are washed away in the waters of baptism; sin and iniquity are burned out of our souls as though by fire; and we become clean, have clear consciences, and gain that peace which passeth understanding." (Spencer W. Kimball, *The Teachings of Spencer W. Kimball*, p. 22.) We can have hope for our child because of the Atonement. "Behold I say unto you that ye shall have hope through the atonement of Christ and the power of his resurrection, to be raised unto life eternal" (Moroni 7:41). Our hope is in Christ and we must never give up that hope.

Before my father died he turned his face heavenward with the happiest, most beautiful smile. Someone leaned over the bed, and asked, "Dr. Rader, how can you smile like that, when there is not one of your children that is serving the Lord?"

He smiled as he answered: "That doesn't matter a bit. It was settled long ago. I brought them up as he commanded me to do. They will every one be brought in. They are a strongheaded group, but God will lead them; yes, every one!"

And every one of them is walking in his way tonight; yes, every one!

Oh, for praying fathers in our nation, and mothers who pray for their children! I tell you, God hears them! He hears! He hears! (Paul Rader as quoted in *The Marriage Affair*, ed. J. Allen Petersen [Wheaton, Illinois: Tyndale House Publishers, 1971], p. 151.)

As long as we are working with our child and loving him and hoping for him, we have not failed him. No one can love a child with such great intensity as a father or mother; so if a parent loses hope, what chance is there for a lost soul? "Oh, parents, no matter what the difficulty, may we never desert our children in some dark and dangerous thoroughfare of life, no matter what prompted them to get there. When they reach the point—and for some it may be a painfully long time—when they reach the point that they need us, I pray that we might not let them down." (Loren C. Dunn, *Improvement Era*, December 1970, p. 64.)

Elder Orson F. Whitney's eloquent plea remains: "Pray for your careless and disobedient children; hold on to them with your faith. Hope on, trust on, till you see the salvation of God." (CR, April 1929, p. 110.)

Elder Boyd K. Packer also adds his concerned petition: "You who have heartache, you must never give up. No matter how dark it gets or no matter how far away or how far down your son or daughter has fallen, you must never give up. Never, never, never." (*Improvement Era*, December 1970 p. 109.)

I never gave up, even though at times it seemed totally hopeless. The few times he came home seemed only to underline his rebellion, because his whole demeanor, physical and mental, exuded his bad attitude.

Although it took many years, one day he pulled it all together and went on a mission. But the real payoff came just a few days before he was to be married (in the temple). This son and I were discussing a young man who had always been considered his best friend, and he stopped me and said, "I don't want to make a big deal out of this, but just for the record, Mom, I want you to know that you are my best friend." What had I done to earn that great accolade? Nothing, really, except that I loved him and never gave up on him.

Charity

Forgiveness is one of the cornerstones of charity. In dealing with a returning prodigal we need only to follow our Lord's example: "Behold, he sendeth an invitation unto all men, for the arms of mercy are extended towards them, and he saith: Repent, and I will receive you" (Alma 5:33). Forgiveness is available to the returned sinner, for "he that repents and does the commandments of the Lord shall be forgiven" (D&C 1:32).

That we must forgive is made abundantly clear in the scriptures. We are required to forgive all who offend us, and if we do not we are guilty of the greater sin (see D&C 64:9–10). As we forgive, we bind the old wounds, soothe the pain, and apply the healing balm of the Atonement to our lives. We can then move forward on our road of eternal progression. President Spencer W. Kimball discussed the theme as follows:

> Another impressive example of unholy judging comes to us in the Lord's parable of the unmerciful servant who owed to his lord ten thousand talents, but being unable to pay, his lord commanded him to be sold, and his wife and children and all that he had, and payment to be made. The servant fell down and begged for a moratorium. When the compassionate lord had loosed him

and forgiven his debt, the conscienceless person straightway found one of his fellow-servants who owed him an hundred pence. Taking him by the throat he demanded payment in full, and upon failure of the debtor, cast him into prison. When the lord heard of the rank injustice, he chastised the unmerciful servant. . . .

According to my Bible, the Roman penny is an eighth of an ounce of silver, while the talent is 750 ounces. This would mean that the talent was equivalent to 6,000 pence, and ten thousand talents would be to one hundred pence, as 600,000 is to one. The unmerciful servant then, was forgiven 600,000 units, but would not forgive a single one.

And again:

"For if ye forgive men their trespasses, your heavenly Father will also forgive you: But if ye forgive not men their trespasses, neither will your Father forgive your trespasses." (Matthew 6:14–15.)

Hard to do? Of course. The Lord never promised an easy road, nor a simple gospel, nor low standards, nor a low norm. The price is high, but the goods attained are worth all they cost. The Lord himself turned the other cheek; he suffered himself to be buffeted and beaten without remonstrance; he suffered every indignity and yet spoke no word of condemnation. And his question to all of us is: "Therefore, what manner of men ought ye to be?" And his answer to us is: "Even as I am." (3 Nephi 27:27.) (*The Teachings of Spencer W. Kimball*, pp. 102, 103–4.)

Forgiveness is a universal need. As to extending forgiveness, to unload such heavy burdens as hatred, anger, wrath, and outrage many will have to go through an intense inward struggle in order to learn firsthand the blessings that result. For those carrying these loads the process is inevitable if they are to enjoy light, hope, and peace.

Conversely, unforgiveness can become a cancer that engulfs us. As we dwell upon our deep-felt injuries the malignancy grows until it overpowers all that is good within us and can destroy our mental, spiritual, and physical well-being.

My friend was a most pleasant and kind lady, a real joy to be with. I always felt a little sorry for her, though, because she was married to a cantankerous man. Finally their marital difficulties deteriorated to the point of which her husband physically assaulted her.

She took her problems to the bishop, who immediately called her husband in. The man confessed that the wife's story was correct. He also expressed a sincere desire to repent and change, and recognized that he would need counseling. He realized the seriousness of what he was doing and was willing to go to whatever lengths were needed to change and to reestablish a healthy and loving relationship with his wife.

His wife, on the other hand, felt humiliated and angry. She felt she had put up with so much for so many years that, although he finally was willing to change, he ought to be punished for all the years of emotional pain he had inflicted on her. She was insistent that counseling and repentance were not enough. The only way her dignity could be restored to her, she felt, was by his being excommunicated. The bishop counseled with her; he told her that the Lord was aware of her situation, that the proper steps had been taken and there would be disciplinary action, but that excommunication was not necessary.

This answer was not acceptable to her. She had come to the Lord and to his servant, the bishop, with a predetermined solution to the problem. Now she felt she had been robbed and betrayed; she had patiently carried this burden for years, and could not imagine any other solution to the problem that would alleviate her grief and pain, would right her wrong. She could not bear that the brethren would not sustain her decision. She left the bishop's office with the promise that she would "have nothing more to do with the Church!" She never came to church again. She divorced her husband and became pretty much of a recluse.

The husband went to counseling and made every effort to repent. We began to see the softening in him; and after a time, he married another lady. She loved to dance and encouraged him to go dancing with her. She bought him new clothes and influenced him to become more outgoing. He became a different man. Instead of being grumpy and irascible, he began to be happy and cheerful, even jolly.

*A few years later, the Relief Society president gave me the special
assignment to be his first wife's visiting teacher. For all those years she
had not allowed a visiting teacher to come into her home, but it was
hoped that, since I had been her friend, she would see me. When I
came to her home, she was out working in her yard. I walked up to her
and started visiting with her. She turned to me and said: "I don't want
to talk to you. Don't try to visit me. I want nothing to do with the
Church or anyone from the Church." And she walked into her house
and shut the door.*

*I was stunned. She had always been such a friendly person, with a
gentle and kindly voice. Now her voice was heavy with anger and bitterness. But what for me was the most amazing circumstance was her
physical appearance. The years of unforgiveness had taken their toll on
her face. That face, which once had been serene and soft, now had become sullen and hard. The bitterness was etched right into every line of
her countenance. No one could look at her without seeing that she was
an embittered and miserable woman.*

Many people have patiently born unjust offenses and, like
the woman in this story, have an honest and legitimate grievance. They come to the Lord with pre-set ideas on what should
be done to solve their problem, and they become angry and resentful when the Lord chooses his way and his time to bind up
the wounds. As in this story, often the perpetrator repents,
moves on, and becomes an outstanding member of the Church,
whereas the victim, allowing his devastation to make him angry,
resentful, and bitter, damns his own spiritual progress. The Lord
has given us the law of forgiveness so that we will be spared
from these negative and unproductive emotions that make us
miserable and impede our progress. The charge to forgive (see
D&C 64:9–10) is a kind commandment from a loving Father
who doesn't want us to suffer needlessly.

Someone hurt you, maybe yesterday, maybe a lifetime ago,
and you cannot forget it. You did not deserve the hurt. It went
deep, deep enough to lodge itself in your memory. And it keeps
on hurting you now.

You are not alone. We all muddle our way through a world where even well-meaning people hurt each other. . . . A friend betrays us; a parent abuses us; a spouse leaves us in the cold. . . .

The great Jewish philosopher Hannah Arendt . . . toward the end of her epochal study on *The Human Condition*, shared her discovery of the only power that can stop the inexorable stream of painful memories: the "faculty of forgiveness." It is as simple as that. . . .

Forgiving is love's toughest work. . . . Forgiving seems almost unnatural. Our sense of fairness tells us people should pay for the wrong they do. . . .

The only way to heal the pain that will not heal itself is to forgive the person who hurt you. Forgiving stops the reruns of pain. . . . When you release the wrongdoer from the wrong, you cut a malignant tumor out of your inner life.

You set a prisoner free, but you discover that the real prisoner was yourself. (Lewis B. Smedes, *Forgive and Forget* [New York: Pocket Books, 1984], pp. 11–12, 170.)

If we do not take the opportunity to forgive, our cancer can multiply and infect the whole family. It can truly devour the productive ingredients that keep us a healthy, functional family. We may not be struggling with the process of forgiving our child, but we may not be able to forgive ourselves, our spouse, other family members, and even well-meaning friends who we feel helped to foster the child's wrongful course.

For many of us the desire to forgive may be there but we don't know how to go about it. Forgiveness is a process; a process that comes inch by inch until we realize that we are at last free from the resentment, bitterness, and pain. It is like lighting one candle at a time in a dark room until all the darkness is gone. Eventually you will be able to see clearly enough to clean out all the cobwebs. If the wound is deep, the healing will take time. Do not become discouraged with yourself as you struggle through the process.

Each person and each circumstance is different. A person who needs to forgive a neighbor for stealing is in a very different

situation from that of the parents or loved ones who must forgive the perpetrator who has stolen their son's or daughter's
virtue. There are even different levels of emotions and circumstances involved when parents need to forgive a child for bringing humiliation and sorrow upon their heads through unyielding
rebellion. Even within circumstances there are circumstances.
But there is one who is an expert on all forms, situations, and
conditions of forgiving—the Savior. He has offered his forgiveness to all, even though it was he who has had to pay for every
kind of wrongdoing imaginable. "And he shall go forth, suffering
pains and afflictions and temptations of every kind. . . . Nevertheless the Son of God suffereth according to the flesh that he
might take upon him the sins of his people, that he might blot
out their transgressions according to the power of his deliverance." (Alma 7:11, 13.)

Nephi explained that we have a resource in Jesus Christ,
after we have exhausted all resources of our own, "for we know
that it is by grace that we are saved, after all we can do" (2
Nephi 25:23). We can reach his help through a deep and sincere desire to forgive. He knows the route that is most suitable
for our personal needs and problems.

Forgiveness and charity together are the path our child will
use to come back to us. If we are unable to forgive, we may find
ourselves being a stumbling block to our prodigal's repentance.

> *There were about seven of us who were caught breaking into a
> store after hours. Since we came from a small, mostly LDS town, the
> police knew all of us and our families. All of the families were strong,
> stalwarts in the Church and community, and held leadership positions
> in both.*
>
> *All of the boys' parents were called to pick up their sons. As each
> of our parents came in, I watched the different reactions as they saw
> their son. Some parents put their arms around their son and said:
> "Let's go home. Don't worry; we'll get through this together." Others
> took the opposite stance. They said, "How could you do this to us?"
> and followed that statement with a good bawling out. My own father
> was among the most loving and kind.*

> Many years have passed, and I have been interested to watch the lives and progress of these youthful buddies of mine. Without exception, the boys who were treated with benevolence and compassion went on missions, married in the temple, and have gone on to Church activity. Among them have been a bishop, a member of the stake presidency, and high council members. Every one of the boys who that night were made to feel sordid and low have completely left the Church.

Few of us have reacted perfectly and calmly in all prodigal situations. Most of us have memories of times when we wish we had handled a family tragedy with more maturity and kindness. Perhaps our unthinking censure has caused a rift between ourselves and our child. Healing that chasm may require some real repair work, but it can be done and the rewards are tremendous. It's true that we can't go back and play out the lost occasion differently, but it's never too late. Although you have shut one door, don't give up. You can open new ones. Maybe you've not shut the door completely. Look for the crack in the door and squeeze through it.

One important reason why we need to forgive is that when our prodigal returns he or she may well bring some untimely baggage. He is going to need our love and our strength in order to work through his problems and find solutions that will best serve him, the family, and the Lord.

> My father never stopped loving me. Once when I asked him if he still loved me, even knowing all he knew about me, he replied, "You are my son, and though you should commit the gravest sin, even murder, I would love you." I never forgot that. It was to my dad that I first broke the news that I had already taken the necessary steps to go on a mission.

It's fascinating, though not surprising since the Lord is consistent, that although separated by time and distance both Paul writing to the Corinthians on the eastern continent and Mormon writing on the western continent understood and taught about charity with inspired cohesion and unison. "Charity suffereth long, and is kind; charity envieth not; charity vaunteth not itself, is not puffed up. Doth not behave itself unseemly, seeketh not her own, is not easily provoked, thinketh no evil; rejoiceth not in iniquity, but rejoiceth in the truth; beareth all things, believeth all things, hopeth all things, endureth all things. Charity never faileth." (1 Corinthians 13:4–8.)

Mormon also clarifies, "charity is the pure love of Christ" (Moroni 7:47). Christ would act with charity if he were in our circumstances. Applied to the task of dealing with a rebellious child, charity means acting as the Savior would act, saying the things we are assured he would say.

> For a son strung out on crack,
>   Charity suffereth long, and is kind.
> For the young man who hasn't held a job in six months,
>   Charity vaunteth not itself.
> For a fourteen-year-old who knows all the answers,
>   Charity is not puffed up.
> For the gossip overheard about a child,
>   Charity thinketh no evil.
> For a child who is rude and abusive,
>   Charity is not easily provoked.
> For the daughter who has just been sent to jail,
>   Charity beareth all things.
> For a runaway who hasn't called for nine months,
>   Charity believeth all things, hopeth all things.
> For the parent who has lost them all,
>   Charity endureth all things.
> For a parent who has just lost one,
>   Charity never faileth.

The relevancy and significance of dealing with willful and even hostile children with Christlike charity is indeed sobering. Our greatest personal goal is to be like Christ. "He that saith he abideth in him ought himself also so to walk, even as he walked" (1 John 2:6).

As so many parents learn, after everything else has been done the only interaction left may be to love the wayward child, to extend Christlike charity. One father said: "Things had reached such a sate that I couldn't reach my daughter. I couldn't talk to her. She ignored rules. Nothing worked. So I did the only thing left—I just loved her."

In this connection there is much food for thought in Elder Marvin J. Ashton's words:

> Real charity is not something you give away; it is something that you acquire and make a part of yourself. And when the virtue of charity becomes implanted in your heart, you are never the same again. . . .
>
> Perhaps the greatest charity comes when we are kind to each other, when we don't judge or categorize someone else, when we simply give each other the benefit of the doubt or remain quiet. Charity is accepting someone's differences, weaknesses, and shortcomings; having patience with someone who has let us down; or resisting the impulse to become offended when someone doesn't handle something the way we might have hoped. Charity is refusing to take advantage of another's weakness and being willing to forgive someone who has hurt us. Charity is expecting the best of each other. (*Ensign*, May 1992, p. 19.)

We cannot extend full and complete charity to our children until we are humble. Pride is the complete opposite of humility. Pride retains every injury, grievance, or unkindness. Humility, on the other hand, sheds, casts off, and lets go of every untoward emotion. C. S. Lewis saw God himself as a great example in this.

> I call this a Divine humility because it is a poor thing to strike our colours to God when the ship is going down under us; a poor thing to come to Him as a last resort, to offer up "our own" when

it is no longer worth keeping. If God were proud He would hardly have us on such terms: but He is not proud, He stoops to conquer, He will have us even though we have shown that we prefer everything else to Him, and come to Him because there is "nothing better" now to be had. . . . It is hardly complimentary to God that we should choose Him as an alternative to Hell: yet even this He accepts. (*The Problem of Pain* [New York: Macmillan Publishing Co. Inc., 1962], p. 97.)

We are drawn to our Heavenly Father and the Savior because of their perfect love. We drop to our knees in prayer knowing that our Heavenly Father deeply loves us and will understand our needs. This is our pattern for parenting. What the wayward child needs from us is our unconditional love.

The parable of the prodigal son demonstrates tenderly how charity, forgiveness, and compassion are tightly woven into a noble character. The comparison helps us comprehend how our Father in Heaven will deal with a repentant rebel. The parable leaves us with no doubts as to God's willingness to meet the sinner halfway to see that he is brought back into the family of God.

> And when he [the prodigal son] came to himself, he said. . . .
>
> I will arise and go to my father, and will say unto him, Father, I have sinned against heaven, and before thee. . . .
>
> And he arose, and came to his father. But when he was yet a great way off, his father saw him, and had compassion, and ran, and fell on his neck, and kissed him.
>
> And the son said unto him, Father, I have sinned . . . and am no more worthy to be called thy son.
>
> But the father said to his servants, Bring forth the best robe, and put it on him; and put a ring on his hand, and shoes on his feet:
>
> And bring hither the fatted calf, and kill it; and let us eat, and be merry:
>
> For this my son was dead, and is alive again; he was lost, and is found. (Luke 15:17–18, 20–24.)

Elder James E. Talmage enhanced our understanding with this eloquent interpretation:

> The father became aware of the prodigal's approach and hastened to meet him. Without a word of condemnation, the loving parent embraced and kissed the wayward but now penitent boy, who, overcome by this undeserved affection, humbly acknowledged his error, and sorrowfully confessed that he was not worthy to be known as his father's son. It is noteworthy that in his contrite confession he did not ask to be accepted as a hired servant as he had resolved to do; the father's joy was too sacred to be thus marred, he would please his father best by placing himself unreservedly at that father's disposal. The rough garb of poverty was discarded for the best robe; a ring was placed on his finger as a mark of reinstatement; shoes told of restored sonship, not of employment as a hired servant. The father's glad heart could express itself only in acts of abundant kindness; a feast was made ready, for was not the son, once counted as dead now alive? Had not the lost been found again? (*Jesus the Christ* [Salt Lake City: The Church of Jesus Christ of Latter-day Saints, 1916], pp. 458–59.)

In dealing with our prodigal we need to emulate the ways of our Savior. This is the secret of charity: Christlike love is pure and unselfish. There is no pride in charity. Christlike love cares not what the neighbors think; Christlike love cares only for the best good of the transgressor. Christlike love attaches no strings and asks no favors. The only condition for our love is to love unconditionally. Always extend charity. The greatest gift is charity, "and whoso is found possessed of it at the last day, it shall be well with him" (Moroni 7:47). Christ asserts, "I have stretched forth mine hand almost all the day long" (Jacob 5:47). His arms are extended to welcome us home in love. We need to have our arms stretched out to welcome our prodigal home "all the day long," or a lifetime, if necessary.

7

Hope on, Trust on

From a grassy knoll I (Janice) sat watching my daughter Julie and her friend Deon at the junior high track meet. Two of Julie's friends were sitting with me, Rebecca and Kathleen. The seventh grade boys had just taken their mark for the 3200-meter race. At the starting gun a young man from our school quickly pulled ahead of the rest. He had a lot of talent and determination, and throughout the race he stayed ahead. If anyone tried to pass him, he would run faster. He was able to keep this up until his final lap. Then another boy passed him, and he couldn't catch up; his strength was spent. A second boy passed him and then another. You could see the disappointment in this young man's face as he finished his last lap. Although he had talent, he lost the race.

The next event was the girls 3200-meter race. There were fifteen girls in the event. Rebecca turned to me and said, "Wendy will win the race."

I asked, "Why?"

"Because she's an Allen," said Rebecca. "Her father coaches her, and her older sister works with her. You know that her older sister Amy took State."

The race started and Wendy set a good pace; every stride was smooth and steady. A few girls passed her from time to time, but her pace remained constant. By the time she began the last lap she was one hundred meters in front of her competition.

We are running the race of life. We too have a Father for our coach, our Heavenly Father. Our Elder Brother took more than a state championship; he took the eternal crown. If we will listen to the word of God and follow the Savior's example, we too can win the race. Why? Because we are the covenant children of God, and his promises are sure and true. This is what Paul did, and he was able to say, "I have fought a good fight, I have finished my course, I have kept the faith" (2 Timothy 4:7).

The Lord has not asked us to run the 100-meter dash using one quick burst of energy. We are in the 3200-meter race. We are going to need to learn how to pace ourselves. The race will be won by the sure, not by the swift. The Lord knows and understands the prodigal's pace and ours. The Lord has assured us that the race will not demand more than we can endure. Elder Orson F. Whitney explained, "God never intended that his work should break men down. He intended that it should build them up." (CR, October 1913, p. 100.) Of the importance of hope to this building-up process, President Ezra Taft Benson has said:

> We must be careful, as we seek to become more and more godlike, that we do not become discouraged and lose hope. Becoming Christlike is a lifetime pursuit and very often involves growth and change that is slow, almost imperceptible. . . . Day by day they move closer to the Lord, little realizing they are building a godlike life. They live quiet lives of goodness, service, and commitment. They are like the Lamanites, who the Lord said "were baptized with fire and with the Holy Ghost, and they knew it not." (3 Nephi 9:20.) (*Ensign*, October 1989, p. 5.)

The race is perilous; of this there is no doubt. We are parenting in the last days, the Saturday evening of time—the experiences of swelling numbers of prodigals and their parents attest to it. This is the hour of extreme polarization: the best and the

worst. Satan rages in the hearts of men, turning the marvels, in-
ventions, and wonders of our age into weapons of mass destruction against our families.

We must carefully tune to and hold on to the still, small
voice that tenderly chaperones us through the darkening mists
of turbulence into the atrium of calm and sunlight. As we contend with the latter-day horrors that are injected into our daily
lives by a careless prodigal, we must be ever watchful that the
latter-day waste by-products of pessimism and negativism do not
enter our lives. President Gordon B. Hinckley likens our situation to the dark days at the beginning of World War II and reminds us we must shun the spirit of pessimism and seek the
spirit of hope.

> Looking at the dark side of things always leads to a spirit of
> pessimism which so often leads to defeat. If ever there was a man
> who rallied a nation in its time of deepest distress it was Winston
> Churchill. Bombs were then falling on London. The Nazi war
> machine had overrun Austria, Czechoslovakia, France, Belgium,
> Holland, Norway, and was moving into Russia. Most of Europe
> was in the grasp of tyranny, and England was to be next. In that
> dangerous hour, when the hearts of many were failing, Churchill
> spoke:
> "Do not let us speak of darker days; let us speak rather of
> sterner days. These are not dark days; these are great days—the
> greatest days our country has ever lived; and we must all thank
> God that we have been allowed, each of us according to our sta-
> tions, to play a part in making these days memorable in the his-
> tory of our race." (Address at Harrow School, 29 October 1941.)
> (*Ensign*, April 1986, p. 4.)

This stern day calls seemingly ordinary parents to magnify
their valiancy. Valley Forge was the crucible that cast George
Washington as the father of our country. The holocaust trans-
figured a quiet spinster, Corrie ten Boom, into a courageous and
tender minister to the victims of depravity. It was the challenge
of the giant Goliath that drew a hero of Israel out of a faithful

shepherd lad. There are many, many ordinary mothers and fathers who will find themselves heroes by rising to the occasion of raising the prodigals of this generation. There is an urgent need today for parents to ascend their own summit. "The power is in them, wherein they are agents unto themselves" (D&C 58:28). Being a parent at the ushering in of the Millennium requires its own special kind of courage.

> There are many in this world who live heroically in simple, daily, faithful service—people often unknown; often unnoticed; often discouraged; sometimes tired and tempted; sometimes feeling they must give up, that they can't go on—and yet they do go on, and, against discouragement, do their duty, daily. . . . And life goes on as well as it does because there are those who do what needs to be done, when it needs to be done, often against difficulty and discouragement. (Richard L. Evans, *Ensign*, January 1971, p. 26.)

President Spencer W. Kimball summed it up in this way:

> To be a righteous woman during the winding-up scenes on this earth, before the Second Coming of our Savior, is an especially noble calling. The righteous woman's strength and influence today can be tenfold what it might be in more tranquil times. She has been placed here to help enrich, to protect, and to guard the home—which is society's basic and most noble institution. Other institutions in society may falter and even fail, but the righteous women can help to save the home, which may be the last and only sanctuary some mortals know in the midst of storm and strife. (*The Teachings of Spencer W. Kimball* [Salt Lake City: Bookcraft, 1982], pp. 326–27.)

Our Heavenly Father understands the skills that are required and the challenges of raising the children of this generation. He knows because he is a parent; a perfect, exalted, glorified, all-seeing, all-knowing, all-loving parent. These are his children too. He yearns for our success and will do everything that the law of agency will allow to facilitate our efforts. And he knows that the parent's task isn't easy. Elder James E. Faust tells us: "The teaching, rearing, and training of children requires more intelligence, intuitive understanding, humility, strength, wisdom, spirituality, perseverance, and hard work than any other challenge we might have in life" (*Ensign*, November 1990, p. 33).

President Gordon B. Hinckley fervently issues the call: "Rise to the stature of the divine within you. . . . 'I am a child of God' is not an idle or meaningless statement. You were there 'when the morning stars sang together, and all the sons of God shouted for joy.' You brought some of that inheritance with you when you came." (*Ensign*, November 1989, p. 95.)

We and our children have been spared for this final harvest prior to the Second Coming. Our Heavenly Father knows us well, and he trusts us to get the job done. Why, then, should we doubt ourselves? Where we are weak, he is strong. His grace will be sufficient, after all we can do. Christ is our strength, our rock. With his help we can endure; we can go on; we can make it.

Let us keep in our hearts those inspiring words of Elder Orson F. Whitney's given at the April 1929 general conference: "Either in this life or in the life to come they will return. . . . Pray for your careless and disobedient children; hold on to them with your faith. Hope on, trust on, till you see the salvation of God."

Index